# The Prestige Press and the Christmas Bombing, 1972

# The Prestige Press and the Christmas Bombing, 1972

## Images and Reality in Vietnam

**Martin F. Herz**

**Assisted by Leslie Rider**

Ethics and Public Policy Center
Washington, D.C.

**Library of Congress Cataloging in Publication Data**
Herz, Martin Florian, 1917-
   The prestige press and the Christmas bombing,
1972.
   Includes index.
   1.  Vietnamese Conflict, 1961-1975 — Journalists.
2.  Vietnamese Conflict, 1961-1975 — Aerial operations,
American.   3.   Journalism — United States.   I.   Rider,
Leslie.   II.   Title.
DS559.46.H47      959.704'38      80-26241
ISBN 0-89633-039-7


$5.00

# Contents

N 1 0 6

# Foreword

THE U.S. BOMBING OF THE Hanoi-Haiphong area of North Vietnam that began on December 18, 1972, was a classic example of a military initiative designed to achieve a political objective. It was also one of the most passionately criticized American actions in that controversial war. The views of supporters of the "Christmas bombing," as it came to be known, were rarely carried in the print or electronic media. In sharp contrast, the *New York Times,* the *Washington Post, Time, Newsweek,* and the three commercial TV networks—the "prestige press"—both lavishly reported the outburst of opposition to the bombing and reinforced it with critical and sometimes scathing editorial comment. This criticism by the prestige media was an extension of their sustained hostility to both President Nixon and the Vietnam War.

The Paris peace talks between National Security Adviser Henry Kissinger and Hanoi's Le Duc Tho had suddenly accelerated in October 1972, when it appeared that an agreement was in sight. Difficulties had then arisen in Saigon, and the negotiations were resumed in November. Then, in December, just when the American side felt that an acceptable agreement had been hammered out, Hanoi hardened its position, and by December 13 the peace talks had become stalemated.

To persuade Hanoi to negotiate seriously, President Nixon on December 14 ordered the renewed mining of Haiphong harbor and the bombing of military targets in the Hanoi-Haiphong area. Four days later the bombing began. It continued daily except for Christmas until December 29, a total of eleven days.

The U.S. prestige press was outraged. On December 20 the *Times* said that "civilized man will be horrified at the renewed spectacle of the world's mightiest air force mercilessly pounding a small Asian nation in an abuse of national power and disregard of humanitarian principles." North Vietnam might yet be bombed "back to the stone age," it said, but perhaps at the price of U.S. reversion to a "kind of stone age barbarism."

Two days later the *Times* asserted that American planes had dropped an estimated 20,000 tons of explosives in the first two days alone—the "equivalent of the Hiroshima bomb"—and asked its readers to imagine what this would do to "New York or any other American city." To stop this "massive, indiscriminate use of . . . overwhelming aerial might," this "terrorism on an unprecedented scale," Americans must "speak out for sanity in Washington and peace in Indochina." (See Appendix D for the full text of this editorial.)

*Times* columnists vigorously supported the editorial position. "How terrible it is to realize this Christmas," said Anthony Lewis, "that in the eyes of most of the world the Christian peace offered by the United States is the peace of the Inquisition: conformity or tormented death." Tom Wicker added: "There is shame on earth, and American shame. . . . Whatever happened in Paris, it is not they who in willful anger are blasting our cities and our people. It is we who have loosed the holocaust."

The *Washington Post* on December 28 called the bombing "the most savage and senseless act of war ever visited, over a scant ten days, by one sovereign people upon another." It continued: "To pretend that . . . we are making 'enduring peace' by carpet-bombing our way across downtown Hanoi with B-52s . . . is to practice yet one more cruel deception upon an American public already cruelly deceived," and "to talk of 'military targets' when what we are hitting are residential centers and hospitals and commercial airports" shows the Administration's "continuing readiness to dissemble." (This *Post* editorial appears as Appendix E.)

After a thorough examination of both the news and the editorials carried by the prestige press, the authors of this study soberly report what really happened on both the military and the political front. There was no "carpet-bombing," no civilian targets were deliberately hit, and according to the official North Vietnamese count, 1,318 civilians were killed in the Hanoi area and 305 in the Haiphong area. This was a far cry from the specter raised by the *Times* and the *Post*—Hiroshima (where nearly 70,000 were killed), holocaust, "terrorism on an unprecedented scale." Unlike

Hanoi's many deliberate attacks against innocent civilians, the Christmas bombing was confined to military targets.

On the political front, the bombing seems to have achieved its principal objective: Hanoi returned to the negotiating table on January 8, 1973, and signed an agreement that led to the cease-fire of January 27.

Although this study examines both the facts of the Christmas bombing and the response of the prestige press, it is primarily concerned with the discrepancy between the two. The authors draw some provocative conclusions about the images evoked by the media and the reality in Vietnam.

The story is told here by Ambassador Martin F. Herz with the calm objectivity that has characterized his earlier works. Ambassador Herz currently teaches at the School of Foreign Service of Georgetown University in Washington and directs its Institute for the Study of Diplomacy. A career Foreign Service officer, he has been U.S. ambassador to Bulgaria and formerly served in Central and Western Europe, the Middle East, and the Far East. He is the author of numerous articles and monographs on recent diplomatic history. Among his books are *Beginnings of the Cold War* (1968) and *How the Cold War Is Taught: Six American History Textbooks Examined* (1978). He is the editor of *Decline of the West? George Kennan and His Critics* (1978). The latter two books were published by the Ethics and Public Policy Center, where for fifteen months Ambassador Herz was a senior research fellow.

Assisting in this project was Leslie Rider, an alumna of Georgetown's School of Foreign Service who is now a graduate student at Columbia University. She formerly was on the staff of the International Rescue Committee in Washington.

This study is enriched by eight appendixes. The first three are U.S. and North Vietnamese statements on the Paris talks and the Christmas bombing. These are followed by three critical comments on the bombing, from the *New York Times,* the *Washington Post,* and CBS News, and by two supportive comments, from the *Wall Street Journal* and the London *Economist.* A brief chronology precedes chapter 1, and names are indexed after the appendixes.

The Center is pleased to make available to scholars and laymen alike this painstakingly prepared case study that illuminates the complexities of wartime policy decisions, the impact of popular passions, and the role of the mass media in a democratic society. The authors alone are responsible for the views expressed.

ERNEST W. LEFEVER, *President*
*Ethics and Public Policy Center*

Washington, D.C.
November 1980

# Vietnam War Chronology, 1972-73

**1972**

March 30   North Vietnamese spring/summer offensive begins with massive attack across the Demilitarized Zone.

April 6    American bombing of North Vietnam resumes.

May 8      U.S. mines Haiphong and other North Vietnamese harbors.

May 23-29  Nixon-Brezhnev summit meeting in Moscow.

June       North Vietnamese offensive peters out, after heavy losses.

June 13    Brezhnev sends Soviet president Podgorny to Hanoi.

June 22    Brezhnev reports to Nixon about Podgorny visit to Hanoi, suggests U.S. propose a date for resuming negotiations.

July 19    Secret Kissinger–Le Duc Tho talks resume in Paris.

July 24    Amendment calling for withdrawal from Vietnam passed by five votes in U.S. Senate (but bill to which it was attached later failed to pass).

Aug. 1     First signs appear of North Vietnamese flexibility in secret Paris talks.

Sept. 15   South Vietnamese retake Quang Tri near the Demilitarized Zone, the only provincial capital the North Vietnamese had captured in their offensive.

Sept. 26, 27  Further concessions by the North Vietnamese in Paris talks.

Oct. 2     Nixon tells Soviet foreign minister Gromyko that U.S. will make "final" proposals to North Vietnamese October 8. If rejected, there will be no further negotiations during election period; afterwards U.S. will return to "other methods."

| | |
|---|---|
| Oct. 4 | Thieu objects to U.S. counter-proposals. |
| Oct. 8 | First "breakthrough" in secret negotiations: Hanoi makes forthcoming proposals, giving up idea of coalition government and accepting continuance of Thieu regime after cease-fire. |
| Oct. 23 | Kissinger goes to Saigon; fails to sell settlement to Thieu, who demands major changes. |
| Oct. 26 | Hanoi "goes public" with the draft settlement and demands that agreement be signed by October 31. |
| Oct. 26 | Kissinger issues "we believe peace is at hand" statement, confirming essential accuracy of text released by Hanoi but stating the clarifications still required. |
| Nov. 7 | U.S. presidential elections: Nixon reelected with 60.7 per cent of vote, to 37.5 per cent for McGovern. However, Senate has larger anti-war majority. |
| Nov. 20 | Kissinger – Le Duc Tho talks resume in Paris. Some progress. |
| Dec. 4 | Le Duc Tho hardens stand, withdraws some concessions, and introduces new changes. Meetings December 6, 7, 11, and 13 show pattern of North Vietnamese "insolence, guile, and stalling." Le Duc Tho says he must return to Hanoi for consultations. |
| Dec. 11 | Thieu appears to reject peace plan in speech to South Vietnamese National Assembly. |
| Dec. 14 | Nixon orders mining of Haiphong and bombing of military targets in the Hanoi-Haiphong complex. |
| Dec. 16 | Kissinger press conference accuses North Vietnam of stalling the peace talks. |
| Dec. 17 | North Vietnamese deny Kissinger's statement about negotiations. |
| Dec. 18 | Bombing of Hanoi-Haiphong area (and of other targets north of the twentieth parallel) and renewed mining begin. |
| Dec. 26 | North Vietnamese send "signal" about resumption of negotiations. |
| Dec. 29 | End ("suspension") of bombing. Agreement to meet January 8. |

**1973**

Jan. 8    Resumption of Kissinger–Le Duc Tho negotiations.

Jan. 9    "Major breakthrough" scored. Tho accepts draft as it had stood November 23, withdraws demands that he had made subsequently, and accepts American compromise language on DMZ that he had rejected in December.

Jan. 12   Negotiations concluded.

Jan. 15   Termination of all bombing and mining activity in North Vietnam.

Jan. 16   General Haig meets with Thieu, explains terms, conveys Nixon message guaranteeing "strong [U.S.] reaction" in case of North Vietnamese violations, threatens that if necessary U.S. will sign alone.

Jan. 20   Thieu accepts the agreement.

Jan. 23   Agreement initialed by Kissinger and Le Duc Tho.

Jan. 27   Agreement signed by North Vietnam, the Viet Cong (PRG) "government," South Vietnam, and the United States.

Jan. 27   Cease-fire goes into effect.

CHAPTER ONE

# Events Leading to the Bombing

## Martin F. Herz

WHEN I WAS OFFERED the opportunity to examine the performance of the prestige media in reporting and commenting on the Christmas bombing in North Vietnam in 1972, I jumped at the invitation because I thought the topic important, interesting, and researchable. I had served in Vietnam (from 1968 to 1970) and have a continuing interest in the subject. I immediately immersed myself in the available material on the military situation, the Paris negotiations, and the American media response to the bombings. But then a strange lethargy set in, which lasted for months. I complained to my wife that I didn't seem able to get a handle on the problem. On the conscious level I wanted to get on with the job. On the unconscious level something was holding me back.

Finally the cause of my frustration became clear to me. I had come to think that the evidence "proved" certain things, but gradually—imperceptibly at first, then almost with a rush—it was borne in on me that these things are, for the most part, quite impossible to prove in any scientific sense: (1) that the bombing, far from creating a new and major obstacle to conclusion of the Vietnam peace agreement, actually facilitated it; (2) that the United States was "unfairly" accused of wholesale slaughter of civilians in the Hanoi-Haiphong area, whereas the bombing was largely confined to military targets and was quite accurate; (3) that the American prestige media—i.e., the *New York Times*, the

1

*Washington Post*, *Time*, *Newsweek*, and the three major TV networks—gave "unfair," one-sided attention to critics of the bombing, failing to present adequately the other side of an important controversy; and (4) that in what was said about the negotiating situation, those media tended to give more credence to the statements of the enemy than to the statements of the government of the United States.

While there is considerable evidence to support all these propositions, I now realize that only the last one is susceptible of proof. The first three run into problems concerning the nature of the information available at the time, the speculative character of assumptions about North Vietnamese motivation, and the logical pitfall of multiple causation, among others, that make it almost impossible to draw conclusions categorically. In my opinion, when one considers the evidence of misreporting and misrepresentation of the bombing and its consequences, one has to be aware that:

1. Before the Christmas bombing, Hanoi was not prepared to sign the agreement negotiated with Washington in October 1972 and improved during negotiations in November. It did sign the November draft, with further improvements (from the South Vietnamese point of view), shortly after the bombing, in January 1973. No one can say with assurance, however, that the bombing caused Hanoi's change of mind. The fact that B happens after A doesn't prove that B was *caused* by A.* I happen to think that the bombing speeded conclusion of the treaty, because I found convincing the statements about North Vietnamese obstruction given by Dr. Henry Kissinger in December 1972, before the bombing began. But unless a member of the Vietnamese Politburo defects and reports that the bombing helped that body make up its mind, the proposition is inherently unprovable. This is so even though subsequent events have shown that those who predicted that the

---

*Neither, of course, can one reasonably conclude, as Tad Szulc concluded in *Foreign Policy*, Summer 1974 (p. 67), and in his book *The Illusion of Peace* (p. 654), that because the agreement signed in January 1973 was only incrementally better than the agreement negotiated in October 1972, *therefore* the bombing had been unnecessary. The argument begs the question. No one can say with any assurance what, if anything, the North Vietnamese were prepared to sign in December.

bombing would cause the North Vietnamese to dig in their heels and harden their stand, or that it would jeopardize détente with China or Russia or both, were mistaken.

2. The bombing was largely done by B-52 bombers, which had never before been used against targets in or near large population centers. The B-52 is widely believed to be an aircraft that delivers its load not on a pinpointed target but over an area, a so-called box measuring about half a mile by a mile and a half. This is the way it had been used on area targets earlier in the war. It was therefore not unreasonable for critics of the bombing to speak of "carpet-bombing," which called to mind the devastation caused by U.S. and British bombing of such targets as Hamburg, Dresden, and Tokyo during World War II. As it turned out, the critics were mistaken. The bombings, for reasons to be explained, were quite accurate, and the loss of civilian lives surprisingly small. But it is hard to fault the critics for thinking otherwise at the time.

3. When the United States was bombing with B-52s, which was done largely at night and through cloud cover during the monsoon season, the precise extent of the damage could be accurately assessed by U.S. authorities only some time after the event. Until extensive photo-reconnaissance could be undertaken, only the North Vietnamese knew precisely what had happened on the ground. They, of course, had no reason to pay tribute to the accuracy of the attackers and ample reason to exaggerate the effects on the civilian population. (The handful of American anti-war activists in Hanoi at the time of the bombing could report only what they were shown or allowed to see, and their reporting turned out to be almost as misleading as that of their hosts.) Furthermore, in the coverage of reactions to the bombing in the United States and abroad, there simply was not much approving comment to report. In free countries, people do not publicly demonstrate their support of an unpleasant military decision taken by their government. The news was largely generated by opponents, and the U.S. prestige media copiously reported as news (with full attribution) the prop-aganda given out by the enemy and his allies. Hence, balanced reporting about the bombing was difficult to achieve. (Difficult, however, does not mean impossible.)

4. The negotiating situation at the time the talks broke down in December 1972 (and whether they actually broke down is itself in dispute) was exceedingly complicated. American officials had raised, largely *pro forma*, various points that President Thieu of South Vietnam wanted them to raise, points that they knew the North Vietnamese would consider non-negotiable. The North Vietnamese had excellent reasons to hesitate and perhaps to draw back from signing the agreement that had been negotiated in October 1972 and clarified and marginally improved (from the South Vietnamese point of view) in November and early December; but they weren't talking about those reasons. The American people, who remembered that Henry Kissinger had in October 1972 declared that "we believe peace is at hand" and who now saw the hostilities being renewed with a vengeance, can be forgiven for wondering if they had been misled by their government.

### The Purpose of This Study

This analysis of media performance is based on the assumption that mass communicators in a democracy have a responsibility to provide a reasonably full and fair picture of major political and military developments. They have an equal obligation to reflect the variety of views about these developments so that the people as citizens can pass judgment wisely on their government's decisions. Those duties are acknowledged in the codes of the print and electronic media. The *Code of Broadcast News Ethics*, for example, states that "broadcast news presentations shall be designed not only to offer timely and accurate information, but also to present it in the light of relevant circumstances that give it meaning and perspective."*

The fairness requirement is more stringent for the electronic media than for the print media because the former must share a limited number of frequencies and channels and are therefore regulated by the government. Under the Federal Communications Commission's Fairness Doctrine, buttressed by law and upheld by

---

*Code of Broadcast News Ethics, Radio Television News Directors Association, adopted January 2, 1966, and amended October 13, 1973, Article Two.

the Supreme Court, all broadcasters are required to serve "the public interest" in their presentation of all public issues. This doctrine is rooted in "the paramount right of the public in a free society to be informed and to have presented to it for acceptance or rejection" the different viewpoints on "controversial issues."* The broadcaster is required to provide accurate news in a meaningful context and has an "affirmative duty" to seek out spokesmen for contrasting opinions and perspectives. When presenting opposing views, the broadcaster must provide a "reasonable opportunity" for each to be heard. Any radio or TV station—and by implication a network—has a right to advocate particular views, but it has a corresponding obligation to present contrasting ones.

While the Fairness Doctrine applies to a station's or network's total public-affairs programming (news, documentaries, and panel shows), the ABC, CBS, and NBC evening news programs with their vast audience and influence have a special responsibility to observe the spirit of balance and fair play embraced in the doctrine. To a considerable extent, I think, the same applies to the *New York Times* and the *Washington Post*, which, as newspapers of record, occupy a special position of trust and influence.

This study takes into account the important distinction between news reporting, which should be as accurate and objective as possible, and commentary or editorials, which, when they are so labeled, may be partisan and opinion-laden. My purpose is not to assemble a bill of particulars against the prestige media for mis-reporting and misinterpreting a significant event in our recent history. It is rather to present the evidence, to tell the story of how top journalists reported and commented on the Christmas bomb-ing. In the final chapter I draw some conclusions. The principal one can be stated here, right at the beginning: Many mistakes were made in communicating the facts and meaning of the Christmas bombing to the American people and the rest of the world. The

---

*FCC 74-702 (18425), released July 12, 1974. A brief history and interpreta-tion of the Fairness Doctrine, which had been evolving for more than four decades, can be found in *TV and National Defense: An Analysis of CBS News, 1972-1973*, by Ernest W. Lefever (Boston, Virginia: Institute for American Strategy Press, 1974), pp. 4-9.

prestige media were not the only ones at fault; the U.S. government had a significant share in these mistakes.

It need hardly be recalled that by 1972 U.S. involvement in the Vietnam War was not popular with the prestige press and the TV news anchormen. In the eyes of the media, the credibility of the Nixon administration was low, even (and perhaps especially) after the President was re-elected in 1972 by a substantial majority. The secretiveness of the Administration, which in the case of the Paris peace talks was necessary, did not make for easy acceptance of its public statements.

## The Christmas Bombing

On December 18, 1972, although nothing in the military situation in Vietnam warranted it, the United States suddenly resumed heavy bombing of North Vietnam north of the twentieth parallel. The attack concentrated on targets in the Hanoi and Haiphong areas; concurrently mines were dropped into North Vietnamese harbors. The next day White House press secretary Ronald Ziegler cited as a reason for the bombing some signs of preparations for another North Vietnamese offensive against South Vietnam; but there had been no mention of such preparations before, and Ziegler's statement had little credibility. Other government sources made it clear that the purpose of the bombing and mining was to force North Vietnam into a more tractable position at the armistice talks in Paris, which had been suspended in disagreement five days before.

This was not the first time during the war that bombing had been used for primarily political purposes, but the occasion was different from previous ones in several respects. First, it had been the general impression prior to the December 13 suspension of the talks between Henry Kissinger and Le Duc Tho that North Vietnam and the United States would conclude an agreement to end the war before Christmas. Two months before, Henry Kissinger, President Nixon's national security adviser, had announced that "we believe peace is at hand" after the North Vietnamese had publicized the text of the agreement—prematurely, to force the

American hand; at that time, according to Kissinger, only minor details still remained to be settled. The massive bombing without *military* provocation was seen by many as a dangerous escalation that could embroil the United States with China, the Soviet Union, or both; and there was widespread disappointment that, instead of peace, the Christmas season was seeing an intensification of the hostilities from which the United States wished to withdraw.

## Background of the President's Decision

To view the bombing in perspective we must look back at the course of the war during the earlier months of that year. The spring and summer of 1972 had seen the biggest North Vietnamese offensive of the war—in fact, the first that pitted two well-equipped Vietnamese armies against each other in "set piece" battles. (The guerrilla component of the war, which continued, had been at a relatively low level ever since the "Tet" offensive in early 1968; a substantial portion of the Viet Cong infrastructure had been destroyed, both during the Tet offensive, when the Viet Cong unsuccessfully attacked the cities of South Vietnam, and during its aftermath, when the South Vietnamese government conducted its "accelerated pacification campaign," 1968-70.) The Communist spring offensive in 1972 involved fourteen regular North Vietnamese divisions and twenty-six independent regiments plus supporting troops, including armor and heavy artillery. It lasted, through several stages, into the summer.

This offensive brought the North Vietnamese only limited successes. Although they overran the northernmost city of South Vietnam, Quang Tri, which was abandoned in panic by its defenders and a good part of its population, that city was eventually retaken by South Vietnamese marines in an eighty-day battle that ended in September. The most lasting success for the North Vietnamese was a widening of their control over the western part of the Central Highlands, which allowed them to establish new logistic complexes along the Cambodian border that would be useful in future operations. In the southern portion of South Vietnam, despite overwhelming superiority in armor and artillery, three

North Vietnamese divisions failed to take An Loc, whose defenders showed astonishing heroism.

On the whole, the North Vietnamese fought with their customary tenacity and disregard for human life; but their losses were so heavy that at the end of the offensive the South Vietnamese, despite their smaller population base, enjoyed numerical superiority over the attackers. For the first time there were also substantial (though still small) numbers of North Vietnamese deserters, and in some retreats the attackers left valuable equipment behind.

In these defensive battles in South Vietnam during the spring and summer of 1972, Saigon's forces could no longer count on American support on the ground, since most American troops had been withdrawn. However, they received massive and very effective support from the air, including strikes by the giant B-52 bombers. For the first time there were clear battle lines, and these heavy bombers could be used with good effect. For instance, they were sufficiently accurate to be used against the attackers of An Loc without hurting the defenders.

The American bombing of North Vietnam, which had been halted, was resumed on April 6. Attacks on military targets in the North became significantly more accurate in 1972 because of the introduction of "smart"—TV- and laser-guided—bombs. For instance, the Thanh Hoa bridge, which had not been hit despite 800 to 1,000 sorties during previous bombing offensives, was destroyed in the first attack. The B-52 operations, however, were not conducted with "smart" bombs but involved targets defined within a "box" of coordinates.

To show its determination to foil the North Vietnamese effort, the United States in May 1972 for the first time dropped mines into Haiphong harbor and other North Vietnamese harbors. President Nixon drew considerable criticism for that action and for the resumed bombing of North Vietnam (which included bombing of the Hanoi area). It was widely predicted that those attacks would lead to retaliation by the Soviet Union or China or both. At the very least, the critics said, the stepped-up attacks would jeopardize Nixon's planned May summit meeting with Soviet leader Leonid Brezhnev in Moscow. But as it turned out there was no such counteraction, and the Moscow summit took place as planned.

According to various reports based on alleged leaks, indiscretions, or unattributed interviews, the Nixon-Brezhnev meeting in May 1972 played an important role in advancing the negotiations between the United States and North Vietnam. (There is no mention of this in either Nixon's or Kissinger's memoirs.) In the "public" negotiations in Paris, the delegation of the Provisional Government of South Vietnam (the Viet Cong, in effect speaking for their North Vietnamese masters) had proposed a tripartite "government of national concord" in which the Communists, the anti-Communist government of South Vietnam, and an unidentified neutralist "third force" would be represented. This proposal had been categorically rejected by the United States and South Vietnam. At the Moscow summit, Kissinger is supposed to have let it be known that the United States would not be opposed to a tripartite body provided its functions were limited to the holding of free elections after an agreed conclusion of the hostilities. Kissinger's office has denied to me that he raised this possibility in Moscow. Whether or not one finds the denial convincing, it is a fact that the idea of a tripartite electoral commission played an important role in the settlement that was eventually worked out between the United States and North Vietnam.

The negotiations, which continued inconclusively through the summer and early fall, brought no progress until late September, when there were significant changes in the positions of the two sides. Since the North Vietnamese had failed in their largest military effort to date, during which an estimated 130,000 of their men had been killed or disabled and vast quantities of their military supplies had been destroyed, they were in no position to resume large-scale hostilities for some time, particularly since resupply had been greatly hampered by the mining of their ports. On the South Vietnamese side, the successful defense had raised the stock of President Thieu—as well as his determination to resist American concessions to his Communist enemies. With Senator George McGovern as the Democratic candidate in the forthcoming elections, the polls showed an increasing likelihood that Nixon would be re-elected. If Nixon could take the considerable risk of mining

Haiphong six months before the election, there was no predicting what he might do after he won re-election.

In this situation, the North Vietnamese made some promising proposals in early October—with the demand that the agreement be signed on October 31, just before the American election. There was extraordinarily rapid bargaining in Paris, and the concessions made by the North Vietnamese were apparent from these features of the draft accord they announced on October 26: they accepted a cease-fire in place, which they had hitherto opposed; they agreed for the first time to a separation between the cease-fire and a political settlement, thus leaving the Thieu government in power; they agreed to internationally supervised elections, which they had repeatedly rejected in the past; and they worked out with the U.S. negotiators the concept of a "National Council of National Reconciliation and Concord" to implement the agreement and to organize elections with the participation of the Thieu government—a pale shadow of their previous insistence on a coalition government. Also, they agreed that the South Vietnamese government could continue to receive American economic and military aid, the latter only on a replacement basis, whereas previously they had demanded that the American withdrawal be followed by a cessation of all American aid to South Vietnam. There were also other provisions that need not be listed in this summary.

## The Paris Negotiations Bog Down

Meanwhile, however, the South Vietnamese government of President Thieu, caught by surprise by the rapid progress in the negotiations, was not ready to settle. It objected to any solution that would permit the continued presence of North Vietnamese troops on South Vietnamese territory (even though this had been implied in all joint U.S.–South Vietnamese cease-fire proposals since October 1970). The South Vietnamese were also intensely suspicious of the idea of a tripartite electoral commission.

To allay Thieu's fears that after an armistice the North Vietnamese would resume their military buildup in South Vietnam in defiance of the terms of the agreement, the United States began to transfer military equipment to South Vietnam that more than made up its battle losses ("Operation Enhance"). This buildup began in the early fall and was accelerated in October. Toward the end of October, however, it became apparent that despite major American pressure and despite the additional arms, South Vietnam would refuse to sign the agreement on the prescribed date of October 31. Worse, an embarrassed Kissinger learned that the Vietnamese-language version of the draft agreement he had negotiated differed in important respects from the English version. The situation was exacerbated by North Vietnamese propaganda describing the (powerless) tripartite council as an interim government.

When it became clear that the Americans could not persuade the South Vietnamese to sign, Hanoi publicly released the terms of the agreement over Radio Hanoi in the early morning of October 26. On the same day (in his "we believe peace is at hand" statement) Kissinger acknowledged the essential accuracy of Hanoi's account but pointed out that some details remained to be settled.

Between October 26 and December 13 three developments unexpected by the North Vietnamese made the situation in South Vietnam less favorable to them. First, many Viet Cong units in South Vietnam, having been led to expect that a cease-fire in place would be announced on October 31, revealed themselves prematurely by seizing or attempting to seize villages and towns that they hoped to claim—only to be captured or killed by the South Vietnamese. Second, the United States, in a further effort to conciliate Thieu, stepped up its "Operation Enhance" into an even larger supply operation dubbed "Enhance-Plus" (involving, for instance, the hurried transfer of American warplanes from the inventories of Taiwan, South Korea, and Iran, at Washington's urgent request). Altogether, the South Vietnamese received about $2 billion worth of arms and supplies in less than two months. Third, when the secret negotiations were resumed in Paris on November 20, Kissinger raised a large number of points that he had promised Thieu to raise, some of them quite fundamental. Although the North Vietnamese rejected most of these points, they initially accepted a few, including one about respect for the DMZ (the demilitarized zone between North and South Vietnam), which made the agreement less attractive to them. Furthermore, some of the discrepancies between the English and Vietnamese texts proved significant and had to be resolved in arduous negotiations.

Another development, perhaps not unexpected by the North Vietnamese and certainly not unwelcome to them, was that there were growing signs that a majority in the new U.S. Congress, which was to convene in January 1973, would favor cutting off all appropriations for the Vietnam war. This prospect tended to weaken the U.S. position in the negotiations. Hanoi's October 26 publication of the nearly completed peace terms increased U.S. domestic pressures on Nixon to settle, even after his re-election.

By early December 1972, the American side—having publicly announced that when it was satisfied with the terms it would sign an agreement even if Thieu would not—expected the agreement to be buttoned up in a matter of days. However, midway in the final phase of the negotiations (or what the United States expected to be the final phase), which began on December 4, Le Duc Tho seemed to have changed his mind on the urgency of an early agreement. He refused any discussion of the protocols of implementation and then submitted new proposals that were entirely unacceptable to the American side. Furthermore, he withdrew several concessions he had made during November and even in early December. It became increasingly apparent that if Hanoi hadn't changed its mind about the desirability of an early agreement, at least it must have instructed its negotiator to play for time so that the Politburo could reassess the entire matter. At the same time, President Thieu—who had been warned that the United States would proceed without him if it concluded that the agreement was reasonable—gained further concessions from President Nixon, notably a personal written commitment that the United States would come to his aid if North Vietnam undertook a wholesale violation of the agreement.

The Paris negotiations ended without agreement on December 13 (the U.S. and North Vietnamese statements on the breakdown are printed as Appendix A and Appendix B of this study), and the U.S. bombing campaign in the Hanoi-Haiphong area began five days later.

## A Personal View

This summary of the events leading up to the Christmas bombing has been, I believe, factual. What follows is my own view of the situation created between October and December.

First, it appears that while President Thieu's continued opposition was embarrassing, it no longer would preclude the signing of the slightly improved agreement between the United States and North Vietnam that seemed within reach at the beginning of December. Second, it seems entirely reasonable that the North Vietnamese were having second thoughts about signing the agreement as it had been amended in November, because four things had happened to make it less attractive: the reduction of their local forces in the South brought about by premature surfacing; the relative strengthening of the Thieu government through operations Enhance and Enhance-Plus; the precisions in the agreement insisted on by Kissinger, which had removed ambiguities, notably about the nature of the National Council of National Reconciliation and Concord; and the prospective changes in the U.S. Congress that would make it worthwhile to play a waiting game. As for Nixon, while the election had strengthened his position, he needed to convince Hanoi that stalling the negotiations would not be to its advantage. Unable to provide its adversary with additional incentives to conclude the agreement, the United States had to find convincing *disincentives* to *non-conclusion*.

I wish to emphasize that unless a credible witness comes forward to tell us, *nobody* can say with any assurance what went on in the North Vietnamese Politburo during the first half of December 1972. It is possible that if the United States had waited, the North Vietnamese would have come back to the peace talks and signed the agreement on the November terms. I do not think so, but the reader need not agree with me.

What I wish to analyze in this study is whether the bombing itself was fairly reported, whether the decision to bomb was discussed on its merits, and whether readers of America's prestige press and viewers of its most influential news programs could gain a balanced picture of what was going on and what was at stake. Answering those questions does not require a particular position on the issues; one need only be aware of the various alternatives.

Since we will be discussing the quality of the reporting and debate, one more point must be brought up at the risk of further complicating an already tangled story. On December 17, just before the bombing began, the North Vietnamese in two broadcasts called for a return to the October draft—i.e., for a jettisoning of all the improvements and clarifications that had been agreed on in the November negotiations. This was not new, but it could have been significant. Reasonable men can differ on whether this offer was serious and whether it should have been accepted. A return to the October draft would have brought an open break between Washington and Saigon (and there were those who thought such a break desirable and necessary). The Administration would have viewed it as a tragedy not only for South Vietnam but also for the United States: it would have involved the betrayal of an ally and a surrender of the improvements that had been arduously won. The debate on the likely costs versus the presumed benefits of such a course of action would have been interesting and worthwhile—had such a debate taken place in the American prestige media.

Very little of the information summarized in this chapter was unknown or inaccessible to the reporters, editors, editorial writers, and TV anchormen and reporters who were presenting the news and expressing opinions on it during the period of the Christmas bombing. But remarkably little was said or written to present a clear rationale for what the United States was doing in North Vietnam. Furthermore, the U.S. government did very little to ward off or minimize the tide of adverse comment that was about to roll over it. This was not unusual. A certain resigned lethargy toward doing battle with the opinion-makers had set in. During the last few years of the war, in the face of what must have seemed the unalterable opposition of the prestige media, the United States government never geared itself up adequately to explain its positions and policies and to rebut criticism on a systematic basis.

CHAPTER TWO

# Reporting by the Prestige Press

## Martin F. Herz and Leslie Rider

ON DECEMBER 16, 1972, two days before the Christmas bombing began, Henry Kissinger gave a detailed explanation of the breakdown of the Paris negotiations. He did not forecast the bombing. This was the last detailed official U.S. statement— except for a list of targets released by the U.S. command in Saigon on December 28—made until after the bombing ended on December 29.

The first news of the bombing came from Hanoi. American officials were tight-lipped on the subject. On December 18, Secretary of Defense Melvin Laird was questioned about the matter during a photographic session where he was preparing to turn over his duties to Elliott Richardson. "After attempting to avoid the question," according to the *New York Times* (Dec. 19), Laird said: " 'Air operations are being conducted throughout North Vietnam at the present time.' He declined to discuss the matter further, saying it might jeopardize pilots' lives." The Administration's silence was all but deafening. The December 19 CBS report on the bombing was based on Vietnamese reports. "From the American side there were few details on the bombing," said the report. "Military sources in Washington and Saigon say President Nixon has clamped a lid on any information. Said one officer, 'We've never been under such tight restrictions.' " On December 22, Robert Pierpont of CBS reported that "pressed to comment on or explain the massive bombing of North Vietnam, Ziegler [the presidential press spokesman] would neither confirm nor deny that it is

15

aimed at forcing Hanoi to accept the U.S. version of a fair settlement." Later, White House press spokesmen answered such questions with "no comment."

There was a reason for this, but it became known only much later. Kissinger had recommended from Paris that the President go on national television to announce and explain the bombing, but the President had refused categorically. Nixon's telegraphed response to Kissinger was: "The thing to do here is to take the heat from the Washington establishment, who know the difference, for stepping up the bombing which will occur for a few days, and simply act strongly without escalating publicity about our actions by what we say about them" *(RN: The Memoirs of Richard Nixon*, New York: Grosset and Dunlap, 1978, p. 730). Nixon's reasoning and the deteriorating relations between him and Kissinger at that time will be examined in chapter 4.

Not surprisingly, the very silence of the Administration was used as an argument against the bombing. News dispatches repeatedly referred to the "secretiveness" of the White House, the State Department, and the Pentagon. Even explanations for the secrecy, when they were given, contributed to the impression that facts were being needlessly withheld. For instance, a report datelined Saigon that appeared in the *Washington Post* as late as December 28 quoted an Air Force major, Gilbert Whiteman, as saying that information was being "temporarily withheld to protect the security of ongoing operations and protect the safety of the crews." This lacked plausibility.

The one White House explanation only made matters worse. On December 19, Press Secretary Ronald Ziegler said: "The President will continue to order whatever action he considers necessary, by air or by sea, to prevent any buildup that could lead to the opening of a new offensive in the South. We are not going to allow the peace talks to be used as a cover to build up another offensive." This implied that the bombing was primarily for military reasons. Ziegler's announcement was immediately followed by a spate of reports that when U.S. military officers were asked whether there had been a change in the recent military assessment that it would take North Vietnam eighteen months to recover from its losses during the spring-summer offensive, they expressed surprise and disbelief.

## Method of Analysis

The factual media coverage of the bombing can be grouped under seven headings: (1) Who Caused the Breakdown of Negotiations? (2) Will the Bombing Achieve Its Purpose? (3) Civilian Damage in North Vietnam. (4) Use of the B-52 Bomber. (5) Foreign Reaction to the Bombing. (6) China: A Special Case. (7) Reaction in the United States. It was especially difficult to distinguish between factual reporting and comment in the period we are analyzing (December 19 to 31), both because of the selectivity of the media in reporting facts and because so much comment was reported in the news columns, in effect giving that comment a free ride as news. But other people's comments *are* news, according to established custom, and it is hard to see where else such comments could have been placed.

We distinguish here between (a) comment in the editorial columns and on the op-ed (opposite the editorials) page, and (b) all material in the news columns. In the analysis of *Time* and *Newsweek*, making this distinction is difficult and involves some arbitrariness, since in those publications news and comment are often intertwined (as indeed they are in television news programs).

The difficulty is compounded when straight editorial comment from abroad is carried in the news columns. For instance, in what category should one place a fairly typical report in the *Washington Post* quoting the London *Daily Mirror* as saying the bombing was "an act of insane ferocity, a crude exercise in the politics of terror, a blunder of tragic magnitude"? Was this comment or news? It was comment reported as news, so we treat it as news. (A single countervailing quote from the London *Daily Telegraph*, also reported in the *Post*, said merely that U.S. actions "may well be right"; this illustrates how one-sided the debate was if one compares the passion aroused in opponents of the bombing to the pained sobriety of its few supporters.)

Another difficulty is the "news analysis" that appears in the news columns. For instance, Carroll Kirkpatrick asserted in the *Washington Post* (Dec. 31) that "secrecy has become a presidential weapon and only the tip of the iceberg is ever apparent to the voters in this democracy." Although this was comment, it was not presented as editorial opinion, so we counted it as part of the news coverage.

We had available complete transcripts of the CBS evening news broadcasts but only summaries of the corresponding broadcasts of the other networks (as published in the Vanderbilt University *Television News Index and Abstracts*). We therefore did not attempt a quantitative analysis of the NBC and ABC news broadcasts. For CBS, we analyzed coverage by lines in the full transcripts, whereas for the newspapers and magazines we used the actual number of printed lines. "Lines" in the five studied sources are not strictly comparable, since the number of words per line depends on the column width and type size. Nonetheless, we think our analysis provides the rough comparability we sought.*

## Who Caused the Breakdown of Negotiations?

The question of whom to blame rose immediately. Considering that the press had abundant anti-U.S. accusations from Hanoi and only sparse information from Washington—except for Kissinger's detailed press briefing on December 16 and one "background" session on December 20—the balance in the news stories is better than might be expected; see table 1.

Line A of the table includes reports that accused the North Vietnamese of having made a fundamental decision against peace

---

*There is a marginal inexactitude in the tallies for the *New York Times* and the *Washington Post*. We counted lines of type but then decided to convert lines into column inches. To do this we used the *Post* measure—a column inch equals five lines—for both newspapers and rounded off to the nearest full inch. By the time we discovered that the *Times* column inch is calculated differently, Leslie Rider had discarded the original line counts. Since we had divided by five to get column inches, we multiplied by five to revert to lines. But since we had rounded off the column-inch figures, the reconstructed line tallies may be one or two lines off. (This explains, of course, why our figures for the *Times* and the *Post* are always multiples of five.)

TABLE 1
ASSIGNING BLAME FOR THE BREAKDOWN OF NEGOTIATIONS
(By lines of text)

|  | N.Y. TIMES | WASH. POST | TIME | NEWS-WEEK | CBS |
|---|---|---|---|---|---|
| A.  Blame Hanoi | 480 | 230 | 134 | 91 | 43 |
| B.  Neutral | 270 | 310 | 44 | 100 | 13 |
| C.  Blame U.S. | 525 | 425 | 58 | 33 | 27 |

or a decision to stall the talks. Reports from South Vietnam that referred to North Vietnamese "perfidy" come in this category. So do reports recalling Kissinger's assertion that the enemy was putting new obstacles in the way of release of American prisoners of war, refusing to discuss the technical machinery of the cease-fire (until the day before he was to return to Washington), and trying to weaken the already weak supervisory force. There were also recollections of Kissinger's charge that the North Vietnamese had withdrawn earlier concessions and had refused to accept language about the DMZ and even a vague reference to some kind of coexistence between North and South Vietnam. This category includes also the report that the North Vietnamese government had "directed an evacuation of women and children from Hanoi on December 4, the day the most recent round of private talks began in Paris" (*New York Times,* Dec. 19), which could be interpreted to mean that the enemy must have known, or at least considered it likely, that the negotiations in December were going to fail or be stalemated. (Actually the evacuation had covered more than women and children; it apparently had not been completed by the time the bombing began.) In a similar and more explicit item on ABC evening news December 21, Howard K. Smith, referring to intelligence reports about the evacuation, added that "U.S. officials theorize that Hanoi may have decided to stall for one or all of three reasons: the expectation that Congress may cut off military aid to South Vietnam; the prospect of further disputes between

Saigon and Washington; or the need for time to prepare a new military offensive." There was no similar theorizing about the reason for the bombing on the CBS evening news.

Line B uses "neutral" to mean, not being impartial toward Hanoi and Washington, but making no value judgments about the behavior of the two sides. This category includes, for instance, both Vietnamese and American denials of the accusations against them, charges that South Vietnam was to blame, attempts to reconcile conflicting claims, and speculative material about the negotiations. Among the latter were attempted explanations of what went wrong in Paris that referred to such sticking points as South Vietnamese sovereignty, the supervisory force, and the DMZ.

Line C includes material that accused the United States of trying to alter the essential principles of the agreement under the guise of technical changes and clarifications. Among the examples are North Vietnamese contentions that the United States had refused to accept the principle that there were two governments and two military forces in South Vietnam and had attempted, instead, to have the armistice agreement establish the sovereignty of South Vietnam. A *Washington Post* (Dec. 31) "news analysis" summarized Hanoi's complaint that among other things Kissinger tried to "make the release of the political detainees in South Vietnam contingent upon the withdrawal of North Vietnamese forces," to "reduce the task" of the proposed tripartite National Council, and to "cancel" all mention of the Provisional Revolutionary Government (Viet Cong) in the agreement, and that he insisted on maintaining U.S. military advisers in South Vietnam under the guise of civilian personnel. The North Vietnamese charged that the United States had proposed 126 changes in the draft agreement—which elicited a denial—and had threatened "on a daily basis" to resume the bombing north of the twentieth parallel. *Time* (January 1, which was on the newstands about December 26) reported that "the last straw" came when the United States reopened a previously settled issue by attempting to establish the DMZ as an *international* frontier, and Hanoi "exploded."

All this is straightforward enough, and the table allows us to note an interesting disparity, which we shall check in the subsequent categories to see if it is a pattern. The ratio of material critical of

Hanoi to material critical of Washington is: *New York Times*, 1 (critical of Hanoi) to 1 (critical of Washington); *Post*, 1 to 2; *Time*, 2.5 to 1; *Newsweek*, 3 to 1; CBS, 3 to 2. CBS had the smallest proportion of neutral items; *Time*'s, too, was relatively small. It should be emphasized again that in this section we are analyzing news, not editorial comment.

## Will the Bombing Achieve Its Purpose?

Assertions that the bombing would be counterproductive were reported widely: it would prolong rather than end the war, it would force Hanoi to stiffen its stand, it would jeopardize détente with Moscow or Peking or both. These were not counterbalanced by reports about the presumed rationale of the bombing, nor even by reports that credited the Administration with a plausible strategy while expressing doubts that it would work. Somehow the news-gatherers seemed able to find only obtuse and unconvincing explanations of what the U.S. government was doing. One report cited a "knowledgeable source" to the effect that President Nixon was hoping to "show Hanoi that he could take the heat at home and abroad" (*New York Times*, Dec. 26), i.e., that he could afford to continue the war. Others said Nixon was demonstrating that he would keep his word by following through on threats made during the talks and by resuming actions previously halted in the hope that Hanoi would display good will and reasonableness in the talks. As a story in the *Times* (Dec. 24) put it, "[as] speculated by some, the President may have ordered the B-52 raids as more of a blunt mauling operation, to show North Vietnam that he has the determination to intensify pressure." There were no reports, or almost none, of the official view that the bombing might hasten the coming of peace.

Views that the bombing was not only cruel and immoral but also futile and self-defeating were reported from Xan Thuy, the North Vietnamese negotiator; a study by a group of leading U.S. scientists under the auspices of the Institute of Defense Analysis; Nguyen Trinh Le, the spokesman for Hanoi's delegation in Paris; anti-war activist Tom Hayden; David Livingston, a New York labor leader; Mme Nguyen Thi Binh, the Vietcong negotiator; "a number of diplomats in Saigon"; "one official" and "an informed intelligence source" in Washington; the Soviet ambassador to France; Hanoi radio; General Vo Nguyen Giap of North Vietnam; "many American experts" who "do not idly dismiss Giap's claim"; the Indian deputy foreign minister; Senator Jacob Javits of New York; three Labor party members (from Coventry) in the British House of Commons; Arthur Galston, a Yale biologist; and others. A great deal of attention—perhaps deservedly—was given to a statement made by a large group of American scientists under the auspices of the American Association for the Advancement of Science; included in the group, in addition to Professor Galston, were three Nobel laureates: George Wald of Harvard, Salvadore Luria of MIT, and Albert Szent-Gyorgyi of the Marine Biology Laboratory at Wood's Hole. There was a preponderance of biologists in the group, and no apparent representation from among experts in politics, strategy, or international affairs.

The disparateness of these sources suggests that reporters sought negative views more assiduously than positive ones. The *New York Times, Time,* and CBS featured about 25 per cent more negative than positive comments about the efficacy of the bombing for pressuring North Vietnam to negotiate, while the *Washington Post* and *Newsweek* devoted three times as much space to such arguments as to the reverse claim that the bombing would or could succeed in altering the North Vietnamese stance.

Looking at these data very tentatively to see if any pattern emerges, we find that for *Newsweek* and CBS the pattern found in the "Who Caused the Breakdown?" section seems to be reversed. The *Washington Post* tends to be more consistent: we saw that twice as much of its news tended to blame Washington as to blame Hanoi for the breakdown of negotiations, and we now see that it gave three times as much space to views that the bombing would be ineffective as to the opposite view.

### Civilian Damage in North Vietnam

What was said about civilian damage caused by the bombing is the most important aspect of this study. It was the most controversial issue. "Balance" in reporting on this point was impossible to attain, since the North Vietnamese and other nationals in Hanoi who sympathized with North Vietnam had a virtual monopoly on factual information and Hanoi understandably emphasized civilian rather than military damage. The U.S. government's denials that it targeted any civilian sites seemed implausible in the face of an avalanche of information that seemed to establish that the United States was engaged in indiscriminate "carpet-bombing."

Throughout the two-week bombing the Administration maintained that it was targeting only facilities of military value. Ten days into the bombing the military command in Saigon issued a press release assessing the damage done to military targets in the Hanoi and Haiphong areas. The list included air bases, railyards and shipyards, SAM (surface-to-air missile) and other anti-aircraft sites, facilities for command and control, for communications, and for vehicle repair, warehouses, power plants, railway bridges, truck parks, and air-defense radar. A mere listing of these targets could not offset the charges that American aircraft, especially B-52s, were sowing paths of destruction throughout civilian areas, killing and maiming on a scale recalling the most intense air raids of World War II. For instance, the statement by the scientists led by three Nobel Prize-winners asserted that the United States

is launching those attacks against concentrated centers of civilian population, while blandly announcing lists of military targets that under these circumstances insult the intelligence of every thinking person. North Vietnam hardly contains military targets; and a B-52 bombing pattern, one and one-half miles long by one-half mile broad, dropped from an altitude of 30,000 feet cannot pick out targets. Yet such bombings are now criss-crossing some of the most densely populated cities of the world, in an unprecedented orgy of killing and destruction that horrifies people everywhere—as Guernica, Coventry, and Dresden once horrified them [statement by the American Association for the Advancement of Science, December 28, 1972].

Subsequent information has established that the bombing was surprisingly accurate and that the number of civilians killed was much smaller than, for example, the number of civilians killed by the North Vietnamese in merely the initial stages of their spring offensive, when they had deliberately aimed artillery fire at thousands of refugees trying to flee southward from Quang Tri. (These matters will be discussed in chapter 4, "What Really Happened.") But information about the accuracy of the B-52 when used as it was used over Hanoi was withheld from the press, as was the fact that military targets near civilian concentrations—for instance, the Hanoi power plant—were bombed with "smart" bombs delivered by fighter-bombers and not subjected to B-52 bombing at all.* An inquisitive journalist could have deduced this from the published target list by noting the category of aircraft assigned to particular targets. But that information, published December 28, was largely ignored.

A blunder by Jerry Friedheim, the Pentagon spokesman, at a press conference December 20 illustrates both the paucity of information about the bombing strategy and the haplessness of military spokesmen in the face of press questioning. Friedheim said first that the United States did not "strike civilian targets" but immediately corrected himself by saying that it did not "target civilian targets." (A *New York Times* editorial—see Appendix D—subliminally transformed this remark to apply to civilian "centers.") Under questioning, he conceded that one could not "rule out" the possibility of collateral damage. When the list of targets was issued in Saigon on December 28, Friedheim "stressed that all the targets on the list of sixty-eight that he released were military ones and that he 'has no reports of any collateral damage' to civilian installations. He conceded, however, that Hanoi is a city like any other, with military and civilian facilities interspersed. Where military sites were targeted, he said, he could not 'rule out the possibility of other things happen-

---

*There were two apparent exceptions. One was the "Hanoi communications facility" listed as a B-52 target. It was also bombed by F-111s and F-4s. According to our reading of military and civilian maps, it is located in the northwest corner of downtown Hanoi. (We are assuming that the "Hanoi communications facility" is identical with the "Hanoi communications office" shown on our maps but could not get this confirmed by military sources. The *New York Times* in a schematic map published on December 28, 1972, assumed they were identical.) Another exception was the petroleum products area in a southern suburb of Hanoi that was among the B-52 targets; it was 200 yards from the Bach Mai hospital. Also close to the hospital were the Bach Mai airfield, a fighter-bomber target, and the "co-located" Bach Mai military storage complex, a B-52 target. An unexplained aspect of the damage to the Bach Mai hospital is that, according to our reading of the aerial photographs released in April 1973, the damage occurred in the part of the hospital complex that was *farthest away* from the Bach Mai airfield and from the petroleum products area.

ing'" (*Washington Post,* Dec. 28). One can imagine the questioning that resulted in his "conceding" that civilians can get hurt when military targets near civilian habitations are bombed.

The predicament of the Pentagon spokesman, obviously under orders not to discuss civilian casualties, can be sensed in the following report:

> To reporters who asked repeatedly about foreign reports of heavy damage and casualties in nonmilitary sections of the capital, Mr. Friedheim said: "You'll have to judge the sources of that information." Pressed on reports of "carpet-bombing" of civilian areas by B-52s he said: "The adjectives you'll have to choose for yourselves. If the implication of your question is that we are bombing civilian areas, the answer is no. . . ." A reporter asked: "Is it your position that you don't want to discuss civilian casualties, and you don't want to tell us the reasons you don't want to discuss the topic, and that any comment is that the North Vietnamese often use such situations for propaganda purposes?" "I'll accept that summation," Mr. Friedheim replied [*New York Times,* Dec. 30].

The news coming from Hanoi stressed damage done to civilian facilities. There were undeniable Western eyewitness reports that the Gia Lam civilian airport had been hit, though it was not on the list of targets. There were reports that Soviet, Chinese, and Polish ships had been hit in Haiphong and that the Cuban, Egyptian, Indian, East German, Bulgarian, Cambodian, and Albanian embassies and the Hungarian trade mission had been hit in Hanoi. (Much later in the bombing, military sources began to suggest that downed American aircraft and spent North Vietnamese anti-aircraft missiles hitting the ground could have caused some of this damage.) There were reports, even alleged eyewitness reports, which later turned out to be vastly exaggerated, that U.S. bombs had damaged the prisoner-of-war facility that the press had dubbed the "Hanoi Hilton." The North Vietnamese charged that the Bach Mai hospital had been "destroyed"; then the American command denied having "hit" the hospital. As it turned out, neither the charge nor the denial was accurate. The hospital, which is located next to a military airfield and military storage facilities, had indeed been hit, but it was far from being completely destroyed. The false denial fueled the fires of exaggerated damage claims.

The report by the North Vietnamese News Agency describing the alleged destruction of the Bach Mai hospital had circumstantial detail that made it quite plausible, especially in the absence of photographic evidence to the contrary, which became available only much later:

> The first bombing attack destroyed a consultation section of the Bach Mai hospital, wrecked the ear-nose-throat institute, and "completely demolished" a research section, Hanoi said. A second B-52 raid Saturday "laid a carpet of bombs of different calibers on a long stretch going from the gate of the hospital to different sections and patient wards," the agency reported.
>
> This strike damaged every untouched room, including underground sections of the hospital, and destroyed the departments of dermatology, internal medicine, pharmacology, administration, kitchens, repair shops, and laundries, Hanoi said [*Washington Post*, Dec. 24].

This report was "corroborated" in an alleged eyewitness account by Telford Taylor, the famous Yale jurist who had been the prosecutor at the Nuremberg war crime trials. Apparently unaware that the hospital was a vast complex consisting of many buildings and wings of buildings, he said flatly that the entire hospital was "blown to smithereens, blown to bits, completely destroyed" (*Washington Post*, Dec. 31). Walter Cronkite (CBS, Dec. 22) reported Hanoi's charge that the hospital had been destroyed and many doctors and nurses had been killed. Taylor also described the "remains of a large low-cost housing development in the An Duong district of Hanoi. Some thirty multiple-dwelling units covering several acres had suffered twenty or more hits leaving fresh bomb craters fifty feet in diameter and virtually total destruction of the homes." The French reporter Jean Leclerc de Sablon (Agence France Presse) provided another eyewitness report on the destruction of the "once busy street" of Kham Thien—near which, he said, the "only" military target was a railway yard that had been "finished off" the week before. The implication was that bombers had targeted a civilian area whose nearness to a railway yard was no longer relevant.

Numerous other claims of high civilian losses made by Radio Hanoi, French reporters, and the Soviet news agency Tass were widely disseminated by the American media. (A North Vietnamese statement broadcast on December 27 that called the bombing raids "brutal acts aimed at massacring civilians" is reprinted as Appendix C.) It is not surprising that in the absence of reliable witnesses to the overall accuracy of the bombing, the media resorted to eyewitness accounts coming out of Hanoi, even when they were patently biased. On December 29, Bert Quint of CBS interviewed an Indian diplomat, Mr. Shashank (presumed spelling), who had just arrived in Vientiane from Hanoi, and another Indian officer. The italics are added to call attention to the similarity between what these "neutral" observers were saying and what Hanoi had claimed.

QUINT: Why are they [Shashank's family] leaving?
SHASHANK: Simply we have seen a state of bombing which was almost unimaginable in the beginning, and things are being bombed without any sort of [unintelligible]. *The civilian targets are being bombed,* and what I'm surprised at, many of these targets are very close to the heavily populated areas of the cities. I have been in Hanoi for the last seven months, but I think first time that I'm seeing this sort of *indiscriminate . . .*
QUINT: Another Indian, a member of the Control Commission, said the bombing is worse than ever. How bad is the bombing?
INDIAN OFFICER: Well, you see, every evening after the bombing is over, you go to the roof of the hotel in Hanoi and you see fire around the town, at least [unintelligible] . . .
QUINT: What about civilians?
INDIAN OFFICER: Very many, very many. They've been dying like anything because I saw one custom officer, in the morning I saw him and in the evening he had died.

Phil Brady of NBC interviewed Shashank and his wife along with the son of an Indian official in Hanoi. Both the line of questioning and the answers are interesting.

SHASHANK: The Bach Mai Hospital, the biggest hospital in the Republic of Vietnam, has been *razed to the ground.* I don't know, people are saying that it has not been hit. But I have seen with my own eyes that it has been hit and directly hit.

MRS. SHASHANK: It's been the worst experience I've ever had in my life I think. I was very scared and I was horrified at it all . . .

BRADY: How bad is the bombing?

MRS. SHASHANK: It's awful. I think all the *military targets have already been taken and now the only thing that is left is the lives of the people, and I think that will be gone as well* . . .

BRADY: Amir's father runs India's embassy in Hanoi, which has already been hit twice by American bombs.

AMIR: It's very bad. They've been coming four or five times a day very regularly. They have six times been coming.

BRADY: Only military targets being hit?

AMIR: No, *there is unrestricted bombing*, they're bombing at every target.

BRADY: How about the North Vietnamese? Has this slowed them down? Are they going to give in?

AMIR: No. The North Vietnamese have been fighting for thirty years. *They're not discouraged at all. And they're going to prove that now to the American people.*

Some resolution of the disparity between the accounts of the U.S. command and those of the eyewitnesses was attempted by *Time,* which recommended that a civilian map and a military map be viewed one atop the other:

> Then it is at once evident that many of those targets lay smack in the middle of the most populous metropolitan and suburban areas in the North. The Hanoi thermal power plant, for instance, was only 1,000 yards from the very center of the city. A main petroleum storage area was only 200 yards from the Bach Mai hospital. The town of Thai Nguyen lay right next to one of the key power plants.

But *Time* did not explain that a map overlay showing the targets of the eight-motored B-52 stratospheric bomber, with its presumed lesser accuracy, would have shown that those targets (with one or two exceptions, as indicated earlier) lay either outside Hanoi or in its outskirts and that this bombing could not have involved either the Hanoi power plant or civilian dwelling areas except by some unintended mishap.

Only one story, the *Washington Post* (Dec. 30), came close to revealing the true disposition of the aerial weapons for different target categories:

Some military sources report that in a few cases the B-52s were used against some targets close to Hanoi where the shock effect of their bombing—with thirty tons of bombs in each plane—could be felt and then the same target was hit again by smaller fighter bombers carrying much more accurate bombs to knock out the target.

This, of course, was still not the full truth, which was that targets in or near the center of Hanoi were generally targeted for bombing by fighter-bombers, which are more accurate than B-52s. Why was this not made clear to the press? Probably it would have provided information that might have been of use to the enemy, for he would then have known where *not* to expect the B-52s, which would have helped him in positioning his anti-aircraft missiles.

The quantitative analysis of news items on bombing damage in North Vietnam that appears in table 2 must be taken in context with the information that follows it.

TABLE 2

News on Military Damage vs. News on Civilian Damage
(By lines of text)

|  | N.Y. Times | Wash. Post | Time | News-week | CBS |
|---|---|---|---|---|---|
| A. Military damage | 525 | 225 | 21 | 20 | 24 |
| B. Neutral | 150 | 220 | 33 | 13 | 71 |
| C. Civilian damage | 1,070 | 610 | 133 | 70 | 91 |

In general, news about military damage tended to convey the idea that the bombing was doing its job, i.e., that it was a legitimate military operation, whereas news about civilian damage suggested that the bombing was indiscriminate and therefore reprehensible. In table 2 the term "neutral" was used for news items that dealt with effects of the bombing but did not fit into either category—for instance, the Pentagon's retort that if the Hanoi prisoner-of-war camp had been hit, then the North Vietnamese were to blame for putting it in an area susceptible to attack; the report that the Gia Lam airport had been hit by mistake; and the Pentagon's suggestion that some of the civilian damage and casualties might have come from crashing planes or unspent missiles. Such items, though not exactly neutral, do not contribute to an impression of either wanton disregard or judicious regard for human welfare.

The proportion for coverage of military damage and civilian damage in news stories in the *New York Times* appears to be 2 to 1, suggesting better balance than in the other media. The reason is that we included in the category "military damage" the 350-line full text of the December 28 communiqué on targets issued in Saigon, which appeared only in the *Times*. A communiqué that lists targets is not really a news story, properly speaking, but a chunk of documentary background. On the other hand, news items about civilian damage, scattered over the entire period and usually featured on the front page, had a much greater reader impact than the 2-to-1 proportion might suggest, even greater from the psychological point of view than the 6-to-1 proportion we would have obtained had the lengthy communiqué not been included.

Overall, news about damage was heavily tilted toward civilian damage—surely in large part because of the availability of such news from Hanoi. It would have required restraint on the part of the prestige media to downplay the abundant news about civilian damage issuing from enemy sources. The proportion in the *Post* is approximately 2.5 civilian to 1 military, in *Time* 6.5 to 1, in *Newsweek* 3.5 to 1, and in CBS news about 4 to 1. (CBS also had a large proportion of "neutral" items.) The overall probable impression of the reader and viewer must have been that most of the bombing damage was done to civilians.

## Use of the B-52 Bomber

The decision to send the B-52 bomber against Hanoi and Haiphong, correctly attributed to Nixon himself, generated considerable debate about the big bomber's limited maneuverability and accuracy. There were thus two issues: Was it wise to expose the B-52 to the concentrated defenses of North Vietnam, where its image of invulnerability would be severely impaired and many American lives would be lost? And was it appropriate and moral to use a "weapon of mass destruction" (which the B-52 was perceived to be) against targets in a heavily populated area? The opponents asserted or implied that the losses in aircraft were unacceptable and that, more important, the B-52 was an inappropriate weapon against targets in a heavily populated area because it was capable only of "carpet-bombing," i.e., bombing a "target box" of a half mile by a mile and a half, as the press kept insisting. To some reporters and commentators the use of the B-52 over Hanoi and Haiphong was a major war crime because in their eyes the main objective must have been to terrorize civilians rather than to destroy military targets.

American losses received great prominence, with Hanoi invariably making exaggerated claims before official U.S. news releases came out. Hence the latter always had to try to overtake and correct the news stories generated by North Vietnam. This was probably inevitable, since Washington had to wait for the return of the planes before making its announcement and since the media reported the first news first. When official American announcements were carried they were sometimes embroidered by the addition of the "price tags" of downed planes. For instance, Walter Cronkite reported on December 21: "The American command now says that in four days since the full-scale bombing resumed, six B-52s have been shot down, *each valued at $8 million."* The cost figure had not been part of the news release but was added by CBS.

The U.S. military pointed out during and after the bombings that the rate at which planes were lost (slightly over 2 per cent per mission) was lower than expected and that the cost-effectiveness ratio was acceptable. But the headline attention given to reports that B-52s had been shot down and the play given to North Vietnamese figures on losses—though always with attribution to the enemy source—created a feeling that the U.S. Strategic Air Command was being bled dangerously over North Vietnam.

On the accuracy of the B-52, CBS claimed (Dec. 21) that "the bombs are considered on target if they fall in a preselected area measuring a half mile wide and almost two miles long." The military insisted that the B-52 was accurate but did not specifically dispute the figures. (The degree of accuracy of the B-52 under ideal conditions—for instance, in "bombing competitions" held in peacetime—is, in fact, still classified information, but of course conditions over Hanoi and Haiphong were far from ideal.)

There were probably inadvertent misrepresentations of the performance of the B-52. The *Washington Post* (Dec. 3), for example, reported:

> For the B-52s to bomb with anything approaching precision, they must stay on a steady course and altitude for at least a few minutes, during which they are good targets [for anti-aircraft missiles]. Trying to maneuver out of the path of these missiles or hurrying their bomb run will throw their bombs off target and would help to explain reports of large-scale devastation to civilian areas in the Hanoi vicinity.

The fact was, as we shall see, that B-52 pilots were ordered under threat of court-martial not to deviate from their prescribed bombing run even when SAMs were coming at them, and as a result many Americans died for the specific purpose of avoiding unnecessary civilian loss of life. Furthermore, it was not true that the bombing run required "at least a few minutes." But even a somewhat shorter period was enough for the computers of the SAM system to figure out where missile and B-52 would meet.

The *New York Times* (Dec. 26) located an unidentified U.S. officer who "acknowledged" that

> without the ground-based navigational aids located in South Vietnam, the bombing was much less accurate. . . . The officer said he believed that the big planes were finally put into large-scale use in the North in hopes that their devastating carpet bombing would deliver a crippling blow to the North Vietnamese.

Actually, the B-52s had a large number of navigational aids that, together with the mode of deployment of the planes, assured a degree of accuracy that compared favorably with that of the bombing of target areas in the South. A quote like this one cannot be checked. The unidentified "officer" might not have belonged to the Air Force. His use of the term "carpet-bombing" makes it highly unlikely that he was informed about the deployment mode of the B-52 in North Vietnam. In fact, his statement was of the very kind that bombing opponents were seeking, perhaps prompting, or possibly even inventing. On the other hand, the *New York Times* (Dec.

22) also carried a statement attributed to "a well-informed officer" that "within the package there were numerous targets, all with assigned priorities, and numerous attack patterns in which several types of aircraft armed with a variety of weapons were being coordinated." This much more than the previous statement reads like something a U.S. Air Force officer might have said.

The self-perpetuating myth that a B-52 inevitably hits an area a half mile wide and one and a half miles long is illustrated by the French reporter Jean Leclerc de Sablon's report that Kham Thien and its adjacent streets "were carpet bombed by planes including B-52s which ploughed up a strip about a mile long and several hundred yards wide from one end of the street to the other" (*New York Times,* Dec. 29). Although destruction from one string of bombs can be observed in aerial photos of the Kham Thien area released in May 1973, this was not "carpet-bombing." The damage observed by M. de Sablon was described in very different terms by later eyewitnesses, as brought out in chapter 4.

Table 3 gives a quantitative breakdown of the news relating to B-52 accuracy and survivability (or inaccuracy and jeopardy).

TABLE 3

NEWS ON THE ACCURACY AND SURVIVABILITY OF THE B-52

(By lines of text)

|  | N.Y. TIMES | WASH. POST | TIME | NEWS-WEEK | CBS |
|---|---|---|---|---|---|
| A.  Positive | 290 | 55 | 3 | 0 | 0 |
| B.  Neutral | 325 | 90 | 25 | 11 | 2 |
| C.  Negative | 135 | 145 | 31 | 34 | 18 |

"Positive material" in table 3 includes any claims of accuracy, statements that the losses were actually lower than anticipated, and also items that acknowledged civilian deaths but termed them incidental. An example of the former would be this *Times* report:

> Pentagon officials insisted ... that targets for the B-52s were being selected so that even if their bombing patterns were slightly off they would not hit civilian centers. For example, they said, the

B-52s might be given a large target of a railroad yard, while targets near civilian centers, such as a bridge or a power plant, would be left to fighter-bombers using precision bombs [*New York Times*, Dec. 22].

An example of the latter is a news item quoting a senior Air Force officer: "Even with the accuracy we get, we're still not sure we would not get a little more than military targets" (*New York Times*, Dec. 31).

Noteworthy is the volume of news on the B-52 in the *Times* compared to that in the *Post*, and also the inversion of the ratio of favorable to unfavorable news (2 to 1 in the *Times*, 1 to 3 in the *Post*). *Time*, *Newsweek*, and CBS had virtually nothing good to say about the B-52 and the decision to deploy it against North Vietnam. The *Washington Post*, in comparison to the almost equally anti-war *Times*, gave greater attention to negative news about the use of B-52s—a characteristic shared in this instance by *Time*, *Newsweek*, and CBS News.

## Foreign Reaction to the Bombing

People rarely demonstrate in favor of an unpleasant decision by their own government—much less one by a foreign government—even if it is regarded as necessary. The coverage in the prestige media of favorable and unfavorable foreign reactions to the bombing is nevertheless startling, as is the thoroughness with which news about unfavorable reactions was sought out and reported. Except for a cursory reference (Murrey Marder, *Washington Post*, Dec. 30) to a "few newspapers in Western Europe" with one citation of a mildly favorable comment, all the papers and broadcasts examined in this study reported positive comment only from South Vietnam, Cambodia, Taiwan, and South Korea. Yet there were doubtless many foreign media, scholars, foreign-policy specialists, and others who supported the bombing.

The avalanche of material about unfavorable reactions recorded views from the Soviet Union, China, Finland, Denmark, Sweden, the Netherlands, Canada, Yugoslavia, Poland, Australia, Singapore, India, Bangladesh, West Germany and West Berlin, and

Belgium, as well as from the Pope, U.N. secretary general Waldheim, Fidel Castro, Catholic peace groups abroad, and the British
Labor party. The reaction ranged from the Pope's relatively mild
expression of "painful emotion" over "harsh and heavy military
operations in blessed Vietnam, which has become a cause of daily
grief" to the assertion by the Polish president of the U.N. General
Assembly that the bombing was "inhuman in all its aspects" and a
statement by Roy Jenkins of the British Labor party calling the
action "one of the most cold-blooded actions in recent history."
The statement of Soviet first secretary Brezhnev on December 21
that the bombing would have an effect on Soviet-American relations was reported by Walter Cronkite (CBS, Dec. 21) as indicating that the "future of Russian-American relations hangs in the
balance." This seems to be an exaggeration of what Brezhnev
actually said, which was: "However—and this should be clearly
emphasized—much will depend on the course of events in the
immediate future and, in particular, on what kind of turn is taken
on the issue of ending the war in Vietnam."

TABLE 4

NEWS ABOUT FOREIGN REACTIONS TO THE BOMBING

(By lines of text)

|  | N.Y. TIMES | WASH. POST | TIME | NEWS- WEEK | CBS |
|---|---|---|---|---|---|
| A. Favorable | 90 | 40 | 3 | 0 | 0 |
| B. Neutral | 60 | 115 | 1 | 15 | 10 |
| C. Negative | 1,010 | 635 | 57 | 16 | 19 |

The overall picture was even more overwhelmingly negative
than table 4 suggests, because of the passion of some of the critical
views reported. The previously mentioned London *Daily Mirror*
comment—"an act of insane ferocity, a crude exercise in the
politics of terror"—was reported in the *Washington Post* (Dec. 30)
with the information that the editorial had appeared on the front
page under the headline "Nixon's Christmas Deluge of Death." In

reviewing mounting worldwide criticism of the bombing, that issue of the *Post* also quoted from *Asahi,* Japan's liberal newspaper: "We believe that what President Nixon is trying to achieve in Vietnam is nothing more than imperialism, colonialism, and genocide." All the media we reviewed reported a statement by Swedish prime minister Olof Palme, a longtime opponent of U.S. involvement in Vietnam:

> What is happening is that a people are being tortured, a nation is being tormented and humiliated to force them to submit to the language of force. That is why the bombings are an outrage. There are many examples of this in modern history. They are usually remembered by names—Guernica, Oradour, Babi Yar, Katyn, Lidice, Sharpeville, Treblinka.

*Time* (Jan. 8, 1973, which was on the newsstands about Jan. 1) carried a quote from an editorial in the French weekly *L'Express* that turned condemnation of the bombing into a personal attack on Nixon:

> In the poker game of life, Mr. Nixon is a master. By means of the nearly blind monster, the B-52, he has discarded forever an assumption. Mr. Nixon is no longer, and will never again be, a respectable man. That is, if he ever was one.

One may wonder whether the news services of the *Times,* the *Post, Time, Newsweek,* and CBS searched as diligently for less condemnatory comment, perhaps from some of the more conservative spokesmen or media in England, France, Germany, and Japan—e.g., *The Economist, Le Figaro, L'Aurore, Frankfurter Allgemeine Zeitung, Mainichi,* or *Sankei Shimbun,* in which editorials less critical of the American president did appear. An analysis in the *Economist* (Dec. 23; see Appendix H) was extraordinarily eloquent in making the case for the American administration. *Newsweek* did quote this comment from *Le Figaro* in its roundup of world reactions (Jan. 8): "As for throwing the entire responsibility for the failure of the talks solely on the American Government, it is good polemics at best."

The "neutral" category in table 4 covers material that noted the restraint of certain official reactions such as those expressed by Western European governments, remarked that reactions seemed slow to develop, or observed that, initially at least, the responses of leaders like the Pope and Waldheim were restricted to expressions of concern.

It is difficult to resist the impression that certain media sought out unfavorable comment for their news columns. The sheer volume of 1,010 lines in the *Times* and 635 lines in the *Post* suggests this, as does the fact that some of the news items came from sources that are rarely quoted in the prestige press. The *Washington Post* (Dec. 28), for example, informed its readers that the Buenos Aires paper *La Opinion* had carried the headline "U.S. Carried Out Most Complete Plan of Destruction in Human History." Similarly, a boycott by Australian seamen, a march of 700 people in West Berlin, and a silent vigil outside the American embassy in London would perhaps not have merited coverage by these media had there not been an effort to build up the picture of American isolation in the world. *Newsweek* reported in its January 8 issue (printed January 1) that "the reaction in most of the rest of the world [had been] immediate and furious," and it spoke of "the outraged reaction among friendly and adversary nations alike." The item was headlined "Diplomacy by Terror."

That the outrage was perhaps not so great and intensive as it might have been was acknowledged at the end of a *Washington Post* story (Dec. 30) headlined "Bombing Criticism Mounts." After devoting 175 lines to reporting protests and criticisms, the *Post* briefly noted: "World press criticism, U.S. analysts noted, has been considerably slower to develop in volume than it did when American troops crossed into Cambodia in April, 1970." Five lines reported a European comment in defense of the U.S. bombing.

### China: A Special Case

Most of the comment about the real, imagined, alleged, or feared effect of the "Christmas bombing" on U.S.-Soviet and U.S.-Chinese relations appeared, quite properly, on the editorial pages or in comment clearly identified as such. This included (as

noted in the next chapter) warnings that détente with the
U.S.S.R. and the development of relations with China could be
jeopardized. But one front-page item merits special attention.
Under the headline "Chou Says Raids Hurt U.S. Relations"
(*Washington Post*, Dec. 29) a report datelined Peking by Mari-
lyn Berger said in part:

> Chou was asked whether the bombing, the second resump-
> tion since he received President Nixon in Peking in February,
> would affect China's relations with the United States.
> His reply, in Chinese, was translated as "Certainly."
> Chou, heaving his shoulders and pointing his finger for em-
> phasis, stopped and said in English: "Surely."
> Asked how the breach could be healed, he said, again in
> English, "Stop."
> Then, in Chinese, he continued: "The United States gov-
> ernment should stop the bombing. I hope you will convey my
> answer to the American people."
> The premier spoke as he passed through the receiving line in
> the Great Hall of the People where some 400 Chinese offi-
> cials, foreign diplomats and journalists were invited to an un-
> usually grand banquet for Mrs. Binh (the Viet Cong "Foreign
> Minister").

It is apparent from this story—and there is more to come—
that the Chinese prime minister had not intended to deliver such
a message to the American people but was "asked" the
question—by the writer of this report—as he was passing
through the receiving line. The question about "how the breach
could be healed" did not refer to anything that Chou had said;
he had not mentioned a breach. The whole statement and ad-
monition were elicited from him by an American journalist at a
social occasion.

Ms. Berger went on to report the glittering function in the Great
Hall of the People where the Viet Cong "foreign minister" was
being entertained. She described in some detail what Chi Peng-fei,
the Chinese foreign minister, had said about the breakdown of
negotiations and the bombing: "The U.S. government committed
a breach of faith, fabricated pretexts, set up various obstacles and
deliberately delayed and sabotaged the signing of the peace

agreement . . .''; the United States was "committing unforgivable new crimes against the Vietnamese people"; and the like. Almost as an afterthought, the story went on to say the following:

> While attacking the United States, he [Chi Peng-fei] also said that China understood that *further talks would be necessary*. "The United States must stop forthwith the bombing of the Democratic Republic of Vietnam," he said, "and *through negotiations*, speedily sign the agreement on ending the war and restoring peace in Vietnam" [italics added].

The contrast between what the Chinese foreign minister was quoted as saying and what the Viet Cong "foreign minister" was saying on the same occasion was glaring—but unremarked by the reporter; for Mme Nguyen Thi Binh was reported as "calling on the United States to sign the draft cease-fire agreement reached in October," i.e., without further negotiation. Considering that the North Vietnamese were accusing Washington of having gone back on the October agreement and that the United States had taken the position that the agreement needed improvement, it is apparent that a *Washington Post* reporter was present on a rare occasion when a major divergence between China and North Vietnam (represented through its Viet Cong satellite) was aired in public. But the *Post*, in its eagerness to report the alleged danger to U.S.-Chinese rapprochement, perhaps inadvertently buried on a back page some news that prefigured the change in the North Vietnamese position that eventually led to an end to the bombing and to the conclusion of the armistice within a month.

## Reaction in the United States

The proportion of unfavorable to favorable news items on American domestic reactions reported in the prestige press is startling, even in the face of the imbalance we have seen so far in the other topics analyzed. The *New York Times* and the *Washington Post* apparently found it almost impossible to locate any favorable comment. Table 5 shows overwhelming attention to critical comment to the virtual exclusion of supportive views.

TABLE 5
NEWS ABOUT U.S. REACTIONS TO THE BOMBING
(By lines of text)

|  | N.Y. TIMES | WASH. POST | TIME | NEWS-WEEK | CBS |
|---|---|---|---|---|---|
| A.  Favorable | 35 | 40 | 5 | 13 | 28 |
| B.  Neutral | 140 | 130 | 30 | 51 | 41 |
| C.  Unfavorable | 650 | 990 | 96 | 75 | 159 |

In all the media there is a telling disproportion; the difference is only in degree. CBS gave six times more space to critical comment than to favorable comment. The *New York Times* had a ratio of 19 to 1 and the *Washington Post* 25 to 1. The news magazines were less unbalanced.

How could such lopsidedness have happened? It might be said that there simply was no favorable comment available. But this seems unlikely when the public opinion polls in 1972 still showed a fairly even division between opponents and proponents of further U.S. support for South Vietnam.

The kind of stories the media highlighted suggests that some support for the President's policy went under-reported. Despite its generous reporting of critical comment on the bombing and its denunciations of the President and of U.S. policy, the *New York Times* (Dec. 23) carried a page-seven story entitled "Reaction to Bombing Is Relatively Mild." It noted that up to then anti-bombing demonstrations were few and that some editors were remarking on the paucity of protest letters. (On the same day Anthony Lewis, writing his op-ed column from London, remarked despairingly on the "inertness of the response in many quarters" in the United States.) But as the thorough reporting on negative comment or action continued, this changed.

Some supportive views were reported, including those of an American soldier, the leader of a prisoner-of-war group, and a smattering of senators. Congressman F. Edward Hebert (D-La.) said he supported the American effort if it would end the war, and

Senator Hugh Scott (R-Pa.) said he was distressed but had hope that the bombing would be successful. William F. Buckley considered the bombing a logical and honorable response to Hanoi's "Mickey Mouse" tactics. The *New York Times* (Dec. 25) reported that the comedian Bob Hope supported the bombing. The *Washington Post* (Dec. 31) reported the assessment of William E. Timmons, head of the President's congressional liaison office, that Congress believed Nixon was really trying to end the war. And that was about all. If, as CBS, the *Post,* and the *Times* (all on Dec. 31) reported, senators polled during the recess opposed the bombing by two to one, then there were more than thirty senators who did not oppose the President's decision; yet their views went unreported.

In contrast, the prestige media reported critical or condemnatory comments from senators Mike Mansfield (D-Mont.), Edward Kennedy (D-Mass.), William Saxbe (R-Ohio), Edmund Muskie (D-Maine), Edward Brooke (R-Mass.), George McGovern (D-S.D.), Clifford Case (R-N.J.), John Tunney (D-Calif.), Harold Hughes (D-Iowa), Jacob Javits (R-N.Y.), Hubert Humphrey (D-Minn.), and Charles Mathias (R-Md.); congressmen Donald Riegle (R-Mich.), Robert Drinan (D-Mass.), Lester Wolff (D-N.Y.), and Edward Koch (D-N.Y.); the Menlo-Atherton chapter of the California Republican League; the Chicago city council; the *Los Angeles Times,* the *Milwaukee Journal,* the *Boston Globe,* and the *San Francisco Chronicle;* Averell Harriman, Theodore Roszak, and Hamilton Fish Armstrong; the Rev. Philip Berrigan, the U.S. Catholic Conference, Rabbi Maurice Eisendrath (president of the Union of American Hebrew Congregations), Robert V. Moss (president of the United Church of Christ), William Thompson (stated clerk of the United Presbyterian Church), Robert Nelson West (president of the Unitarian Universalist Association), and "the social action directors of the seven provinces of the Society of Jesus."

These critical statements did not lack forcefulness and pungency. The moral concerns of the nation were said to be reflected in a statement by "an interfaith group of forty-four religious leaders" that denounced the bombing as "an unspeakable assault upon this season's message of peace on earth" (*Washington Post,* Dec. 23). One of the most frequently cited negative reactions was the defection of Senator William Saxbe (R-Ohio) from the Nixon camp and the termination of his longstanding support of the Administration's Southeast Asian policy: "I have followed President Nixon through all his convolutions and specious arguments, but he appears to have lost his senses on this." Saxbe was also quoted as saying the decision to bomb Hanoi and Haiphong demonstrated "arrogance and irresponsibility."

An NBC interview (Dec. 26) gave Senator McGovern an opportunity for an unusually long statement in which he said in part:

> In the last ten or eleven days we've seen the most murderous aerial bombardment in the history of the world—the first use of B-52s, the largest bombers we have, in North Vietnam. I think this policy has not only destroyed any immediate hopes for peace, but I think it's the most immoral action that this nation has ever committed in its national history. It's made a travesty of the whole spirit of Christmas. . . . We're bombing in one of the most densely populated sections of Indochina, in the outskirts of Haiphong and Hanoi, where most of the people have fled in order to get away from the central cities. It's a policy of mass-murder that's being carried on in the name of the American people. And I hope the people of this country will rise up against it.

It may be noted that the senator acknowledged that B-52s were bombing not the cities proper but their "outskirts," but because he placed the bulk of the population of Hanoi and Haiphong in the outskirts, he made the bombing appear as a calculated effort to destroy civilians. (In this suggestion McGovern was unique among opponents of the bombing.) Senator Harold Hughes was quoted as declaring: "It is unbelievable savagery that we have unleashed on this holy season; the only thing I can compare it with is the savagery at Hiroshima and Nagasaki." Senator Mike Mansfield said on ABC news: "I think that bombing will just put steel in their backbones and prolong the war." Senator Jacob Javits said: "The North Vietnamese have not been bombed into a settlement, and there is nothing to indicate that our renewed air strikes are going to have that effect now." A statement by Senator Mathias quoted in the *Washington Post* summarized many of the concerns that motivated the protests and calls for congressional action:

> Even if the bombing is successful in bringing the parties back to the negotiating table . . . the price would be too high in lives lost . . . and the highest of all in our loss of moral leadership in the world.

As in the case of reports on reactions from abroad, the coverage of unfavorable comments by American leaders included some whose importance—particularly in the absence of any countervailing items of even moderate importance—might be questioned. Among these were the views of the president of the First National Bank of Boston, seventy-eight activists picketing the home of Nixon's New Jersey campaign chairman, and clergymen who picketed the White House (and thus got featured on the CBS evening news).

Our review of reporting about U.S. reaction leads us to the conclusion that with a minimum of effort, the prestige media could have reported more comment from people who, while perhaps not enthusiastic about the bombing, would not have been so sharply critical as those whose views were reported. These could easily have been found among the many American scholars, historians, and foreign-policy specialists who supported the Christmas bombing as a means for persuading Hanoi to negotiate more seriously.

CHAPTER THREE

# Comment by
# the Prestige Press

## Martin F. Herz and Leslie Rider

IN OUR SOCIETY THE CRUCIAL distinction between reporting the news and commenting on it is accepted in theory and
frequently violated in practice. The standards for responsible reporting are spelled out in the various broadcasting and print media
codes. They focus on a balanced presentation of facts and views
about significant events or developments. But there are no similar
requirements for editorials, in which opinions about events can be
freely given, though under the FCC's Fairness Doctrine, as noted
in chapter 1, a broadcaster is required to label comment as such
and to provide a "reasonable opportunity" for diverse opinions to
be aired.

The following analysis of the prestige media's editorial performance takes these distinctions into account. The views of the *New
York Times* and the *Washington Post* toward the Vietnam War
were well known, and it would have been surprising had those
papers—or Walter Cronkite on CBS—had anything good to say
about the Administration's handling of the negotiations or about
the bombing in December 1972. No one can criticize an editorial
writer for voicing strong opinions.

However, the confidence with which editorial writers and columnists assumed certain assertions about the Christmas bombing
to be facts is, in retrospect, remarkable. This combined with the
selective news reporting that we examined in the previous chapter
created a continuing one-sided influence on elite public opinion.

## Opinions in the *Times*

The first *Times* editorial on the bombing ("Deception or Naive-té?," Dec. 19) was scathing on all counts. The bombing "is not likely to hasten—and could indefinitely postpone—the 'just and fair' agreement that Henry Kissinger has said is the President's objective," said the *Times*. Furthermore, Washington was at fault for the breakdown of the negotiations:

> But it was Washington that introduced Mr. Thieu's substantive demands into the Paris talks, upsetting the tentative agreement that had been hammered out in October and opening the way to counterdemands from the other side. It is President Nixon, according to all available testimony, who is now insisting that a final accord somehow require Hanoi to recognize that Saigon is to remain in control of the South.
>
> However devoutly to be wished, this is an unrealistic condition that attempts to impose at the peace table a political solution that has not been won—and cannot be won—on the field of battle.

The *Times* ridiculed Kissinger for having said that his call for language in the agreement that would "make clear that the two parts of Vietnam would live in peace with each other and that neither side would impose its solution on the other by force" was "a modest requirement," "relatively easily achievable." (That Kissinger said he would have settled for a vague formulation, "however allusive, however indirect," was not mentioned.) What, asked the *Times*, did President Nixon and his advisers think that the history of Vietnam for the last eighteen years had been all about? The paper said that Nixon and Kissinger had been "either deceptive or naive in their pre-election assurances to the American people about the imminence of peace in Vietnam." And it concluded by saying, "Peace was not at hand, and Mr. Kissinger has given no convincing reasons for believing that it was." So the implication was conveyed that Kissinger, whom few have accused of naiveté, had deliberately deceived the American people.

This was only the opening salvo of what became a drumfire of scathing comment. The alleged indiscriminate character of the bombing and its brutality were assumed. The next day (Dec. 20), the *Times* accused Nixon of "resorting once more to naked force" and commented that "civilized man will be horrified at the renewed spectacle of the world's mightiest air force mercilessly pounding a small Asian nation in an abuse of national power and disregard of humanitarian principles." North Vietnam may yet be bombed "back to the stone age," as an Air Force general once suggested, said the *Times*, but "in the process, the United States itself is in danger of being reduced to the kind of stone age barbarism that could destroy some of what is most worth preserving in American civilization."

In "Terror From the Skies" (Dec. 22; reprinted as Appendix D of this study), the *Times* said that "normally" B–52s operate in flights of three that lay down a pattern of bombs—twenty tons to a plane—"which scatter over an area more than half a mile wide and more than a mile and a half long." Claiming (quite erroneously) that American planes had dropped 20,000 tons of explosives in the first two days alone, the paper said that this was the "equivalent of the Hiroshima bomb"—implying that tens of thousands of civilians were being slaughtered. "Imagine what would happen to New York or any other American city," the *Times* said, "if a comparable enemy force were unleashed to attack such targets on the Pentagon's authorized list as railyards, shipyards, command and control facilities, warehouse and transshipment areas, communications facilities, vehicle-repair facilities, power plants, railway bridges, railway rolling stock, truck parks, air bases, air-defense radars, and gun and missile sites." The reader would be likely to suppose that the bombing was destroying Hanoi and Haiphong. The editorial concluded resoundingly:

> No matter who is to blame for the breakdown in talks, this massive, indiscriminate use of the United States' overwhelming aerial might to try to impose an American solution to Vietnam's political problems is terrorism on an unprecedented scale, a retreat from diplomacy. . . . In the name of conscience and country, Americans must now speak out for sanity in Washington and peace in Indochina.

On the same day, the *Times* reported on an editorial from *Le Monde* (Paris) that compared the bombing with the atrocity at

Guernica during the Spanish civil war and spoke of "covering this dense crowd with a carpet of bombs," concluding that North Vietnam was being "martyred" by an "abomination" because Nixon was bypassing the U.S. Constitution "by the logic of an imperial system." As noted in chapter 2, *Times* columnist Anthony Lewis (Dec. 23) deplored the absence of a public outcry against "a policy that many must know history will judge a crime against humanity." What was the purpose of the bombing? he asked: "It is only, Henry Kissinger says, to make sure the American departure is 'honorable.' For that we have caused, are causing and presumably will continue to cause the most terrible destruction in the history of man."

The emotions of Christmas were intermingled with opposition to the war and the bombing in columns by Lewis, "Good Will to Men" (Dec. 25), and Tom Wicker, "Shame on Earth" (Dec. 26). Lewis said:

Americans are used to regarding themselves as the good neighbors of the world, innocent and helpful. How terrible it is to realize this Christmas that in the eyes of most of the world the Christian peace offered by the United States is the peace of the Inquisition: conformity or tormented death.

And Wicker:

There is no peace. There is shame on earth, and American shame, perhaps enduring, surely personal and immediate and inescapable. Whatever happened in Paris, it is not they who in willful anger are blasting our cities and our people. It is we who have loosed the holocaust.

On December 24, a *Times* article by Leslie Gelb and Anthony Lake claimed that Nixon was seeking a North Vietnamese "surrender" and with the bombing was "lashing out at North Vietnam like a spoiled child who cannot get his way." On December 27, the paper exhorted the Congress to put an end to the war by linking further funds to the achievement of a settlement and the return of the prisoners of war. On its op-ed page were the appeal of the scientists mentioned in chapter 2 and an article by General Maxwell Taylor, who argued that there was no need for any written agreement to withdraw the remaining American forces.

## Opinions in the *Post*

The *Washington Post* did not lag behind the *Times* in vigorous condemnation of the bombing. It accepted as fact virtually everything that Hanoi and the American anti-war movement were claiming. A long editorial entitled "The Great Peace Charade" (Dec. 19) made two somewhat contradictory points: that Kissinger had been naive or disingenuous in ascribing "some dark and dubious bargaining tricks" to the North Vietnamese, since he of all people should have realized that they "are not behaving like perfect gentlemen"—and that he had craftily tried to trick the North Vietnamese into conceding, under the guise of a minor amendment to the agreement, the crucial point of the whole war, namely "nothing less than the political future of South Vietnam." The paper concluded that this, rather than any alleged North Vietnamese obstruction, had transformed the entire negotiating process into a "charade." The opposed objectives of North and South Vietnam, the editorial said, cannot be reconciled: "there is no conceivable settlement short of an unwinnable victory." The President must "accept this harsh reality"—and, presumably, withdraw from Vietnam on North Vietnamese terms.

Like the *Times,* the *Post* did not accuse Kissinger outright of deception in his "peace is at hand" statement in October, but it came so close that the effect was the same. It said, first, that a charade was a game that "takes two teams to play," adding that "Mr. Nixon and Dr. Kissinger have made their own considerable contribution to this particular charade." Referring then to Kissinger's October statement, the *Post* said: ". . . it is important to remember that the critical piece of pantomine, if you will, was played out on television on the eve of the national election, with the most careful calculation, with what had to be enormous political effect." The implication was clear: Kissinger had been less than truthful. At the least, the paper said, "he and the President have been taken for a long hard ride by the North Vietnamese; in short, they have been had, by Dr. Kissinger's own admission." But the reason for this was not artfulness or duplicity on the part of the

North Vietnamese; it was the fact that the American negotiators had made unrealistic demands.

In "Terror Bombing in the Name of Peace" (Dec. 28; reprinted as Appendix E) the *Post* called the bombing "the most savage and senseless act of war ever visited, over a scant ten days, by one sovereign people upon another." It argued that there could be no resolution to the fighting that would yield more than ambiguity:

> To pretend that we are doing otherwise — that we are making "enduring peace" by carpet-bombing our way across downtown Hanoi with B-52s—is to practice yet one more cruel deception upon an American public already cruelly deceived. It is, in brief, to compound what is perhaps the real immorality of this administration's policy—the continuing readiness to dissemble, to talk of "military targets" when what we are hitting are residential centers and hospitals and commercial airports; to speak of our dedication to the return of our POWs and our missing in action even while we add more than seventy to their number in little more than a week.

This paragraph epitomizes the *Washington Post*'s stance. The *Post* accepted it as fact that the United States was, as North Vietnam was claiming, "carpet-bombing" residential areas of Hanoi; it accused the Administration of "cruel deception" about the causes of the breakdown in the negotiations; it was convinced—as we saw in its December 19 editorial—that the bombing would not lead to an agreement; and it disbelieved the Administration's statements that our bombers were *aiming* only at military targets. The editorial called the bombing "the heaviest aerial onslaught of this or any other war," thus conjuring up the idea that the casualties must be on the order of those inflicted on Dresden, Tokyo, and Hiroshima (though a parallel with those World War II bombings was not explicitly drawn). The pattern was clear. The *Post,* like the *Times,* had for years given greater credence to enemy claims about the war than to statements issued by U.S. officials— not always without justification.

While editorially as scathing and denunciatory as the *Times,* the *Post* had nothing to match the eloquence of Lewis and Wicker on its op-ed page. Most of its columnists, while hostile to the bombing, were analytical and prescriptive rather than outraged and condemnatory. Among the guest columnists during this period was former ambassador Charles W. Yost (Dec. 30), who saw "the cruel and foolish" resumption of the bombing of North Vietnam as "throwing détente into hazard." The détente with the Soviet Union and China had removed, he wrote, "the only convincing reason for the United States' concern with a Vietnamese war, which was originally conceived of as an instrument of their expansion. One can therefore say that rarely in history has so much been risked for so little."

Among the regular columnists, Victor Zorza (Dec. 20) hypothesized what no one could possibly have known: that Hanoi made the original October concessions "after a fight in which the hardliners were narrowly defeated by Communist 'doves.'"

> It took the Hanoi Politburo three days to digest the reports from Paris, and to take a new vote on the new American demands, which went far beyond what had been previously agreed. In these circumstances, the Hanoi hardliners would have been able to argue that they had been right all along, and to swing the Politburo majority to their side.

Zorza concluded that Nixon's very "unpredictability" had become predictable and that Hanoi would now try to exploit a hypothetical split that was developing between a Nixon "hard line" and a softer line allegedly sought by Kissinger.

Another *Post* columnist, Kenneth Crawford, decided that "Kissinger, a Most Unlikely Victim, Was Had" (Dec. 23). Crawford did not share the view held by Senator McGovern (and strongly implied by the *New York Times*) that the original "peace is at hand" announcement had been a deliberate hoax. Rather, he held that Kissinger had been led down the garden path by the Communists, who never intended to settle with the Americans. When Kissinger had tried to clarify the deliberate obscurities of the October agreement, Crawford argued, "the Communists went into their pettifogging, obfuscating, nerve-jangling act. Anyone who has ever seen this performance, even in a communist-infiltrated organization, must sympathize with Kissinger. After his October optimism, they had him set up for the double cross."

Crawford's conclusion was that on the one hand, public opinion would force the *American* government back to the negotiating table, i.e., that the North Vietnamese were reaping tactical advantage from the bombing; and that, on the other hand, if the bombing was the right tack now, "then it was a mistake to discontinue [it] as a gesture of good will while the Paris negotiations were proceeding." The implication of the column was that a test of wills was involved in which the United States, notwithstanding North Vietnamese weakness, would lose because of the pressure of public opinion to settle on enemy terms.

But "Hanoi Was Had" according to an infrequent contributor to the *Post,* Josiah Lee Auspitz (Dec. 24). Auspitz asserted that Nixon had never wanted a reasonable agreement; realizing belatedly that the agreement Kissinger had negotiated would bring the downfall of Thieu and the vindication of McGovern, the President was now doing "the ugliest thing Americans have seen a President do for many a Christmas." Another infrequent contributor, Fred Bronfman, wrote at length about the hideousness of the American ordnance dropped on North Vietnam, some of it designed to "penetrate underground shelters," some employed for maximum effect on human bodies, and so on (Dec. 24). Bronfman claimed that the use of plastic in bombs was especially reprehensible because, North Vietnamese doctors said, "the fragments do not show up on an X-ray." (The *Post* later carried a Pentagon statement denying that any American bombs used plastic for shrapnel, although some of the fins on bombs were made of plastic for aerodynamic effect.)

Murrey Marder (*Washington Post,* Dec. 23) took the position that since Kissinger and the North Vietnamese had diametrically opposing explanations for the breakdown of the negotiations, and since the facts were not known, "the opposing arguments must be taken on faith. But blind faith disappeared years ago—an early casualty of the war." In other words, Marder at least left open the possibility that Hanoi might not be telling the truth. Columnist Stewart Alsop (Dec. 27) asked: What would Nixon do if the North Vietnamese refused to return to the conference table? "Nuke Hanoi? Hit the dikes? Or just go on bombing North Vietnam till hell freezes over?"

## The Other Prestige Media

It is more difficult to identify editorial or columnist comment in the news magazines and the networks because in these media news and comment are often intertwined. *Time* (Dec. 25) gave the Kissinger side of the controversy about the breakdown of the negotiations but remarked that "the U.S. may be demanding more, *in Hanoi's view,* than has been won on the battlefield." (Italics in comments in this paragraph are added to highlight "hedging.") It concluded that "the American people had every right to feel disillusioned and *perhaps* even misled." In the next issue (Jan. 1, 1973), *Time* called the bombing "brutal" and noted that "the B-52 is better at saturation bombing than pinpoint attack: Hanoi's claim of high civilian casualties was *propagandistic but plausible.*" Writing like this makes it difficult to categorize the editorial position. The same was true of *Newsweek.* It asked such questions as, "Was Kissinger's 'peace is at hand' declaration just before election day only a political gambit?" (Dec. 25). In its January 1 issue, it reviewed the chronology of the negotiations and their breakdown and noted that "the savage, wrenching turnabout on the path toward a settlement confirmed the belief of many Americans— *well founded or not*—that they could not trust their own government." Although *Time* and *Newsweek* did not *support* Washington's position, their comment was distinctly less negative than what was said in the *New York Times* and the *Washington Post.*

To identify "editorial" opinions in the transcripts of the CBS afternoon and evening news shows is difficult, since those shows consisted almost entirely of visual news stories. Many stories were negative: the pronouncements of war critics, reports about the families of prisoners, Communist and other foreign denunciations of the United States, reports of protests in America, and the like. But this comes under the heading of selective news reporting rather than direct editorializing. The only outright CBS editorials were those of Eric Sevareid, whose technique, as required by the medium, is "cool" and thus for the most part one of indirection and implication. Such "comment" cannot be analyzed in depth here; the tone is apparent in the following Sevareid passage (Dec. 22):

The great government buildings here have gone dark; the traffic crawls along in the cold drizzle as the people who man this government head for their homes and the long Christmas holiday. The air of dejection here compares in some measure at least with the Christmas of '41 when our navy lay smashed at Pearl Harbor and the night when everyone thought the war in Europe was all but over, and learned instead that the Nazis had smashed back in the Battle of the Bulge and peace again receded. The high hopes of early autumn are in ruins. In most areas of this government, the very high levels included, the feeling is one of dismay, tinged with shame that the United States is again resorting to mass killing. [The] credibility gap is opening wide, and unless there's a resolution quickly, a good many reputations will slide down its slopes. The sense of shock has not yet turned into organized protest, partly because it is the holiday season. The Congress is out; the colleges are closed. We know little of what is happening in North Vietnam, save what Hanoi Radio claims. American military authorities are held to virtual silence, and the President himself maintains total silence. . . . If serious and productive negotiations are not resumed, then the haunting question is, What higher bargaining cards or weapons do we possess? Does the will exist to use them; and at what cost to the Asian country and to ourselves?

The picture is one of almost unrelieved gloom, with the question of more intensive pressure on North Vietnam (nuclear weapons?) raised subtly. In a subsequent comment (Dec. 29; reprinted as Appendix F) Severeid was somewhat more outspoken:

Is it possible to get what the President calls an honorable peace by dishonorable means? How is it possible to preserve American leadership and credibility in the world, which the President says is the important goal, when the moral base for that national posture is being hacked away?

To raise questions in such rhetorical terms is to answer them.

CHAPTER FOUR

# What Really Happened

## Martin F. Herz

DURING THE ELEVEN DAYS of the bombing of North Vietnam, December 18 to 29, 1972 (there was no action on Christmas day), the United States dropped over 20,000 tons of bombs on targets in the Hanoi-Haiphong area. This was by far the largest and most concentrated bombing campaign of the war. In tons of ordnance dropped, the operation can be compared to some of the heaviest bombings of World War II. There were 724 sorties by B-52s (most of them carrying thirty tons of bombs) and 640 strike sorties by other aircraft (A-7s, F-4s, F-111s) plus 1,384 sorties by other aircraft (reconnaissance, SAM/flak suppression, escort, combat air patrol, electronic countermeasures, search and rescue, and others).

Despite the magnitude of this effort, the number of civilians killed in Hanoi, by the official North Vietnamese account of January 4, was 1,318. The number of wounded was given as 1,261. (The number killed in Haiphong was 305.) Much as one must deplore the loss of civilian lives—indeed, of all lives—in a war, the extraordinary aspect of these figures is that they were so low, considering the intensity of the bombing effort. There is simply no comparison with the civilian toll taken by the major bombing raids in Germany and Japan during World War II.

That the number of dead must have been small became apparent during the bombing campaign but was overlooked or downplayed by the media. For instance, on December 21 the *New York Times* carried on its front page a report from the Soviet press agency Tass charging that the raids had caused "heavy" civilian casualties and damaged "thousands" of homes; many pages later—on page 16—there appeared an inconspicuous Associated Press report that Hanoi had claimed only 260 deaths in Hanoi and Haiphong as a result of the massive raids up to that time.

## Why Civilian Deaths Were Low

Among the reasons for the exceedingly low number of fatalities are these:

1. Hanoi's civil defense measures were effective. Mayor Tran Duy Hong explained to a *Washington Post* reporter on February 4, 1973: "When American bombs struck in December, two-thirds of the population had been evacuated. This explains why despite the B-52s few people were killed." The evacuation continued after the bombing began, so that by the end of December probably three-quarters of the population had been evacuated.

It is interesting, incidentally, to note that the mayor of Hanoi reported after the armistice (*Washington Post,* Feb. 3, 1973) that in December he had received advice from American "comrades" to claim a figure of 10,000 dead but that he had refused, saying this would harm North Vietnamese credibility—so that, if the United States later really killed 10,000 persons, "nobody would believe us."

2. B-52s were assigned to "area" targets outside Hanoi and Haiphong proper or in their outskirts;* the more precise and accurate fighter-bombers were used on targets in or near densely populated areas. Despite charges of "carpet-bombing" by B-52s inside Hanoi and Haiphong, targets such as the Hanoi power station were given not to B-52s, which bombed at night by radar, but to smaller planes that bombed visually by day. The power station was attacked and destroyed by one flight of F-4s using "smart" (laser-guided) bombs during one of the very short periods of good visibility.

---

*As noted earlier, the Hanoi communications facility may well have been an exception to this rule.

This is not to say that B-52s were never used against targets that were near civilian concentrations. In several instances B-52s were assigned "area targets," such as the Kim No storage area and the Hanoi petroleum products area, that, though on the outskirts of the city, were still close enough to civilian installations—such as the Bach Mai hospital—that collateral damage occurred, apparently from bombs released by error or accident. The town of Thai Nguyen, located next to the Thai Nguyen electric power plant, falls into a slightly different category. It sustained major damage and loss of civilian life through repeated efforts to put the power plant out of commission; the question arises whether it would not have been better to wait for the weather to clear so that the plant could be attacked with "smart" bombs launched by fighter-bombers. (It appears, in fact, that after the B-52s failed to destroy the thermal power plant, F-111s were called in to complete the job.) But clearly targets within heavily populated areas or close to such centers were, with one or two exceptions, not assigned to B-52s. This point was made clear by the target list. (And if that list had been faked the media would undoubtedly have found it out.)

Despite the insistence of sources in the Strategic Air Force that the B-52 is superior in accuracy to fighter-bombers, there is no doubt in the minds of the authors of this study that the fighter-bombers (even when *not* using "smart" bombs) were more accurate than the stratospheric B-52Ds, whose huge mixed load of 108 bombs of 750 and 500 pounds had a substantial amount of scatter during descent. According to Guenter Lewy, it has been estimated that in 90 per cent of all B-52 missions one or more bombs landed outside the target "boxes" because of bent or damaged fins (*America in Vietnam*, p. 412).

3. Another factor in the low civilian damage was the particular mode of bombing ordered for the B-52s. This information was not given out during the bombing and subsequently became available only through specialized publications, such as the U.S. Air Force monograph "Linebacker II: A View from the Rock." Without going into classified information, it can be said that the "cells" of B-52s were smaller and more concentrated than those observed by the press in previous bombings, such as the bomb-

ings around Khe Sanh in 1968 and around An Loc in the summer of 1972; that planes in the cells did not necessarily drop their bombs at the same moment; and that the operation took place under instructions that minimized civilian casualties through the lines of approach selected for bombing runs, through strict instructions to refrain from evasive action against Hanoi's surface-to-air missiles (SAMs) during the bombing runs, and through orders to withhold bombs and jettison them into the sea if prescribed target accuracy could not be assured.

To be sure, the threat of court-martial against aircraft commanders who maneuvered to avoid SAMs during their bombing runs was not motivated only by a desire to minimize civilian casualties: it was also caused by a concern for "cell integrity," because of the fear of collisions and also because staying close together made the planes' electronic countermeasures against the SAM guidance systems more effective.

Altogether North Vietnam launched more than 1,250 SAMs. The United States lost twenty-six aircraft, including B-52s, all SAM victims. The loss of B-52s was slightly over 2 per cent, which is well below the loss ratio of bombers in World War II. It is known that many SAMs exploded in the air without hitting their intended targets, and also that many failed to explode and headed down again. Some of the damage in populated areas that was attributed to U.S. planes in general or to B-52s in particular was likely to have been caused by huge SAMs and other anti-aircraft ordnance that fell to the ground without hitting their targets. (Incidentally, it appears that by the time the bombing was stopped upon receipt of a signal from North Vietnam that it would resume negotiations, the enemy had fired its entire stock of SAMs; continued bombing by B-52s would therefore have been much less risky for the attackers.)

### The Damage to Hanoi

Eyewitness accounts, some even during the bombing, contradict the claims of "carpet-bombing" and indicate that the accuracy of the attackers must have been quite remarkable, considering the magnitude of the bombing campaign. Malcolm W.

Browne of the *New York Times*, a confirmed critic of the Nixon administration's conduct of the war, reported from Hanoi after the January agreement that "the damage caused by American bombing was grossly overstated by North Vietnamese propaganda" (March 31, 1973). After a visit in March 1973, Peter Ward of the *Baltimore Sun* wrote that "evidence on the ground disproves charges of indiscriminate bombing. Several bomb loads obviously went astray into civilian residential areas, but damage there is minor compared to the total destruction of selected targets" (March 25).

Tammy Arbuckle of the *Washington Star,* who visited Hanoi in late March 1973, reported: "Pictures and some press reports had given a visitor the impression that Hanoi had suffered badly in the war—but in fact the city is hardly touched" (April 1). Arbuckle was not shown the Bach Mai hospital but managed to visit Kham Thien, the area about which the French News Agency had reported so luridly in December, and described the destruction there as follows:

> We were shown Kham Thien. It looked as if about 60 houses had been destroyed and another 20 damaged. North Vietnamese officials said about 215 people were killed at Kham Thien. It was difficult to assess what sort of bombing had caused the destruction as makeshift houses have sprung up on the ruins of the old.

The Kham Thien area, according to North Vietnamese sources (*Washington Post,* Feb. 4, 1973), had a population density of 75,000 persons per square mile. Although many of these must have been evacuated, the low official number of dead in this residential area suggests that it was not "carpet-bombed" by B-52s.

Telford Taylor, who had reported in December that the Bach Mai hospital had been "blown to smithereens" and implied that the destruction had been deliberate, modified his assessment after a second visit. The *New York Times* (Jan. 7) quoted his revised view that the bombs that hit the hospital "were probably directed at the airfield and nearby barracks and oil storage units." In his earlier report Taylor had not mentioned the hospital's proximity to these military targets, or if he had, the point was censored by the North Vietnamese. (It is interesting that, despite these revised reports, the charge of deliberate attacks on civilian targets was accepted as true by Dale S. DeHann, counsel to the Senate subcommittee on refugees, who visited Hanoi in March 1973, and by the chairman of the subcommittee, Senator Edward Kennedy.*)

Not until April 4, 1973, inexplicably, did the Defense Department release aerial photographs to prove it had not engaged in "carpet-bombing." The *New York Times* reported this in an article by Drew Middleton entitled "Hanoi Films Show No 'Carpet-Bombing'" (May 2). The key passage follows:

> Aerial photographs of the results of the heavy United States bombing of Hanoi last December show damage to military targets, to a hospital near a military airfield, and to a commercial and residential area close to the main railroad station and yards. The photographs, taken by reconnaissance drones after the twelve-day bombing offensive and made public by the Defense Department, include one composite picture of Hanoi. This does not support charges made during the offensive that United States Air Force planes subjected Hanoi to the kind of carpet-bombing employed against German cities in World War II.

The article noted that the damage to the Bach Mai hospital, which had been the focus of much international criticism, was explained by the hospital's proximity to the Bach Mai military airfield, which was heavily bombed by B-52s, F-111s, and F-4s: "The runway was cut at two points and ten support buildings and ten barracks were destroyed. But what were described as premature bomb drops severely damaged several buildings in the nearby Bach Mai civilian hospital." The pictures, according to Middleton, also showed some heavy damage in the Kham Thien area near the railway yards, but the *Times* writer reported that there was no evidence of deliberate bombing of civilian areas. However, the *Times*, whose editorials had complained about wholesale devastation, did not acknowledge these findings in its editorial columns.

As for the *Washington Post*, it tucked the information about

---

*U.S. Senate, Committee on the Judiciary, Subcommittee to Investigate Problems Connected with Refugees and Escapees, *Hearings on Relief and Rehabilitation of War Victims in Indochina*, Part III: North Vietnam and Laos, July 31, 1973, 93rd Congress, 1st Session, 1973, p. 72.

what the aerial photographs revealed at the end of a news story about another subject ("Cambodian Peril Is Discounted by Pentagon," April 5) on page 24. Of course, this paper, which had specifically charged carpet-bombing "across downtown Hanoi," did not comment on the new information; and the other media surveyed here did not even report it incidentally.

There is another oddity about the aerial photographs. They were presented to the House Defense Appropriations Subcommittee on April 4, but when Admiral Thomas Moorer, the chairman of the Joint Chiefs of Staff, was asked why this information had not been revealed before, he said (according to the *Post*) that "the large photo wasn't available until January" and that "cease-fire negotiations were going on again at that time." It is difficult to see why release of the photo intelligence about the actual extent of damage in Hanoi would have interfered with the negotiations, which in any event were concluded on January 12. It is also difficult to understand why, with the photo intelligence available on April 4, the *Times* reported it only on May 2. One can speculate that perhaps there was some reluctance that had to be overcome.

## The Nixon-Kissinger Disagreement

Why, during the Christmas bombing and for some time thereafter, the U.S. government was silent about the objectives of the bombing and said so little about the steps taken to minimize civilian deaths, is no mystery. As noted in chapter 3, the silence about objectives resulted from a decision by President Nixon taken against the repeated advice of Henry Kissinger. The interplay between these two men on this point as reported in their memoirs is noteworthy. Both Nixon and Kissinger reported that when it looked as if the talks would have to be broken off and the bombing resumed, Kissinger recommended that the President go on television to enlist the support of the American people for the stern measures that would be taken. "I believe that you can make a stirring and convincing case to rally them as you have so often in the past with your direct appeals," Kissinger telegraphed from Paris (*RN: The Memoirs of Richard Nixon*, New York: Grosset and Dunlap, 1978, p. 726). But the President disagreed.

Instead of a frantic and probably foredoomed attempt on my part to rally American public opinion behind a major escalation of the war, I preferred an unannounced stepping up of the bombing. This would be coupled with a press conference by Kissinger to explain where we stood in terms of the new attempts at reaching a settlement, and why the negotiations had broken down [ibid.].

Kissinger disagreed and remonstrated, but Nixon notes: "I remained unconvinced of the wisdom and the feasibility of this course of action" (p. 727). Later, in a telegram, the President told Kissinger: "I have talked to a few of the hard-liners here in total confidence, and it is their strongly unanimous view that it would be totally wrong for the President to go on TV and explain the details of why the talks have failed" (p. 728). Kissinger describes his own state of mind at the time in this way:

> If I admired Nixon's decision [to break off the talks and resume the bombing], I was less enthusiastic about his refusal to explain it to the public. . . . *But Nixon was determined to take himself out of the line of fire* [italics supplied]. I was asked to give a low-key briefing of the reasons for the recessing of the Paris talks; how to be low-key about such a dramatic event was no more apparent to me in Washington than it had been in Paris. I had no objection to this assignment; indeed, I volunteered for it. But if there was a major uproar, only the President would be able to quiet it and give the public a sense of where we were headed. It was proper that I should be the butt of attack, as I had been and would be again the focal point of success. . . .
>
> But the overriding, immediate need would be to calm public fears and rescue national self-confidence out of the bedlam certain to follow Nixon's decision. *Nixon explains that he was concerned not to jeopardize the negotiations; silence enabled him to avoid giving our actions the character of an ultimatum and thus permitted Hanoi to return to the conference table without loss of face* [italics supplied]. This was part of his concern; but I also think there were other, more complex reasons. Nixon was still seized by the withdrawn and sullen hostility that had dominated his mood since his electoral triumph. He resented having to face once again the emotional travail of an expanded war at the very start of his new administration. He was much less certain of success than I; he told me his doubts repeatedly [*White House Years,* Boston: Little, Brown and Co., 1979, pp. 1448, 1449].

Personally I believe that Nixon was right and that a campaign to rally the American people behind their government at the time of the Christmas bombing would have failed. Such a campaign should have been started much earlier, and sustained throughout the war. If the Administration had fought back, it would not have reversed the tide of public opinion, but it would have given heart to its supporters and probably increased the number of the undecided. Similarly, information to disprove the charges of "carpet-bombing" could have been released earlier if the Administration had not virtually given up on the prestige media.

The memoirs reveal a distinct difference between Nixon and Kissinger in their inclination to compromise. The President was not only loath to confront the American public with an explanation for the bombing; he was also less certain that the United States should persevere in trying to improve the October agreement.

The record of messages as reflected in the two memoirs shows quite clearly that Nixon was more eager than Kissinger to settle on minimum terms, i.e., on the basis of the earlier, virtually concluded agreement. In late November he cabled Kissinger that "we must recognize the fundamental reality that we have no choice but to reach agreement along the lines of the October 8 principles" (*White House Years,* p. 1421). The next morning, however, he reversed himself. Kissinger reports that he telegraphed the President that "I did not see how we could accept returning to the October text (not to speak of one even worse, as Hanoi proposed). Though I considered the agreement a good one then, intervening events [obviously, the tabling by the United States of Thieu's requested changes] would turn acceptance of it into a debacle" (p. 1429). But as late as December 10, General Alexander Haig, Kissinger's deputy, cabled from Washington that "if even this [compromise] fails, the President, as we predicted, *would even be willing to cave completely* with the hopes that we can still bring Thieu around" (p. 1439; italics added).

However, the North Vietnamese went into a stall and effectively halted the negotiations in the second week of December. Clearly, Hanoi had developed doubts about the whole enterprise. No one can say what would have happened if the United States had not proceeded to bomb the Hanoi and Haiphong areas and to resume the mining of North Vietnamese ports. However, the fact that the agreement concluded the following month, January 1973, was from the point of view of South Vietnam better than the October draft—it included all the improvements and clarifications obtained in November and early December—suggests very strongly that the bombing influenced the North Vietnamese decision to settle on a mutually satisfactory basis.

Some readers will wonder whether any of this matters, since eventually the North Vietnamese won the war. But they won it only in 1975, after many other things had happened, including the weakening and demoralization of the United States and South Vietnam caused by Watergate and the congressional cutback of funds for military aid to Saigon, both of which emboldened the enemy to launch the final offensive.

CHAPTER FIVE

# Images vs. Reality:
# Seven Conclusions

## Martin F. Herz

As we draw conclusions about the performance of the prestige media in reporting and commenting on the Christmas bombing in Vietnam, it is important to recall the responsibility of the press in a free society. We cannot and do not expect perfection from journalists, newspapers, and TV news programs, which generally must operate with tight deadlines and without all the facts. But American citizens have a right to expect a reasonable degree of fairness, balance, and honesty from their major sources of news. The broadcast media should strive to live up to the Fairness Doctrine and their own industry codes. While the print media are not obligated by law to be fair in reporting contrasting views, they too have codes that call upon them to provide a balanced picture of the day's news.

These were the general standards we used to analyze *Time, Newsweek,* the *New York Times,* the *Washington Post,* and the CBS thirty-minute evening TV news program. I freely acknowledge that content analysis is far from being an exact science, that an element of subjectivity is always present. But I believe that any competent person going over the same material with ordinary standards of fairness would come to approximately the same conclusions.

Long before the controversial bombing of December 1972, most of the prestige media were clearly on record against U.S. involvement in the Vietnam war: they saw it as a mistake, as an exercise in futility, or even as a crime. (*Time and Newsweek,* while sharply critical of the Christmas bombing, were previously less hostile to U.S. involvement than the *Times,* the *Post,* and Walter Cronkite of CBS evening news.) Therefore to say that these media opposed the Christmas bombing is to state only the obvious. Their opposition was explicit in the daily newspapers, implicit for the most part in the network news broadcasts.

Moreover, one did not have to be an inveterate opponent of U.S. involvement to suspect that the B-52 was an inappropriate aircraft for bombing in or near major urban areas in North Vietnam or to question whether this bombing was an appropriate response to the breakdown of the Paris talks. But the facts adduced by the prestige press in support of their position were often wrong. There was no "carpet-bombing," and the bombing did not stiffen Hanoi's stand in the negotiations, any more than the bombing campaign in the spring had stiffened its stand. The bombing was much more accurate and politically effective than the critics—and also, perhaps, some members of the Nixon administration—had expected. All this is by now pretty obvious. Less obvious are the following observations.

1. The editorial position of the prestige press doubtless affected the selection of news stories on the Christmas bombing. This is more true of the *Times,* the *Post,* and CBS News than of *Time* and *Newsweek.* Granted, supporters of an unpopular military action do not usually feel strongly enough about their position to demonstrate in its behalf; opponents of the action are more apt to advertise their position and their availability for comment. But even when allowance is made for this, it is clear in retrospect that the news reporting was highly selective. None of the prestige media managed to find much positive reaction. Six times as much negative as positive U.S. reaction was carried by CBS News and *Newsweek,* nineteen times as much in *Time,* twenty-one times as much in the *New York Times,* and twenty-five times as much in the *Washington Post.* And in the coverage of foreign reactions, the ratio was 11:1 in the *Times,* 16:1 in the *Post,* 19:1 in *Time,* and no favorable items at all in CBS News and *Newsweek.* Yet much comment favorable to the Administration's decision was available, both abroad and

at home. It is hard to escape the impression that the reporters or editors selected and sought news unfavorable to the government and made little effort to seek out comment with which they—or their bosses (or their ideological peers)—disagreed. An example is the comment elicited from Chinese premier Chou En-lai, who till then had refrained from such pointedly adverse comment.

Open editorial comment is the media's privilege and responsibility; but the record presented here raises the question whether the deliberate shaping of news, the seeking out and stimulation of comments that buttress the political position of the particular medium, does not violate journalism's own standards. It appears to me to be a dubious practice, especially in a time of national crisis. Comment must always be free, but editorializing through news-making and news selection seems to me to be a surreptitious means of influencing the reader and viewer and may thus be damaging to the free formation of opinion that is important to a democracy.

2. The *Washington Post* was consistently the most negative toward the U.S. position. In reporting about reactions to the Paris talks, the *Times* carried roughly an equal number of stories condemning Hanoi and stories condemning Washington. The *Post,* presumably working with the same material, devoted twice as much space to newsmakers who blamed Washington as to those who blamed Hanoi. In reporting comments on the likely efficacy of the bombing in bringing peace, the *Times, Time*, and CBS had pro and con items in rough balance, whereas the *Post* and *Newsweek* (the latter is owned by the *Post*) reported three times as much negative as positive comment in their news columns.

3. The relative silence of the U.S. government in stating its case on the negotiations and the bombing deprived the media of some information that would have enabled them to present a more balanced picture had they been so disposed. This tight-lipped posture during the crucial December 18 to 30 period was, as we have seen, adopted against the advice of Henry Kissinger. There may have been some merit in the position Kissinger attributes to Nixon, that "silence enabled him to avoid giving our actions the character of an ultimatum and thus permitted Hanoi to return to the conference table without loss of face," but the silence in De-

cember 1972 was only an extreme of what had prevailed for some time. The Nixon administration never made the major effort required to do battle on a continuing basis with the prestige media and the ideological opponents of U.S. involvement in Vietnam. Even so, despite the government's virtual silence, supporters of the decision to undertake the bombing campaign did not find it impossible to present a plausible defense of that action. (Two examples appear as Appendixes G and H.)

4. The propositions that the bombing was effective in bringing the North Vietnamese back to the conference table and that it contributed to the early conclusion of the armistice in 1973 cannot be proved or disproved. But the hypothesis that by early December the North Vietnamese had lost interest in the negotiated agreement is plausible when one reviews the salient facts in the situation at that time. Certainly they seemed eager to come to terms after the bombing, an eagerness they had conspicuously failed to display before. (Whether their "loss of face" would have been significantly greater if Nixon had given a public explanation of the rationale for the bombing is another question that could be answered authoritatively only by a high-ranking North Vietnamese defector.) At any rate, those who predicted that the bombing would delay conclusion of the treaty were wrong.

5. There is no evidence that the U.S. Air Force engaged in the "carpet-bombing" of civilian centers. Such charges, which were prominently featured in the prestige press, were without foundation. The credibility accorded to Hanoi propaganda by key sectors in the prestige press and the bias of these media against U.S. involvement made it almost inevitable that Hanoi's charges would be presented as fact. But as we noted in chapter 1, even unbiased persons could reasonably believe that use of the B-52 automatically meant "carpet-bombing." In any case, the distorted reporting led to the unfortunate situation in which the U.S. military were continually trying to correct falsehoods and exaggerations that had been printed or broadcast. American "peace" activists who were in Hanoi at the time contributed to the distortion, sometimes unwittingly. It is hard to see why the U.S. Air Force waited three months to present proof that there had been no carpet-bombing of Hanoi.

In this instance, again, the U.S. government did not defend itself well against its critics.

6. Judged by accepted practices of warfare, the Christmas bombing was not disproportionate; much less was it a "war crime." In every war the question is properly raised as to whether a particular military action is excessive, measured by the objectives it was undertaken to achieve. The principle of "proportionality" is an integral part of the classic doctrine of the just war. Telford Taylor, former chief counsel at the Nuremberg War Crimes Trial and an opponent of U.S. involvement in Vietnam, throws some light on this problem. In a lecture to the Columbia University Club of Washington (Feb. 21, 1980), he addressed the charge that the United States sought to destroy Hanoi:

> Despite the enormous weight of bombs that were dropped, I quite rapidly became convinced that we were making no effort to destroy Hanoi. The city remained largely intact, and it seemed quite apparent that if there were an effort to destroy Hanoi it could have been done very readily in two or three nights. So I think any suggestion that the object of the raid was to wipe out or raze Hanoi is quite mistaken.

Taylor stated that the bombing of North Vietnam under the circumstances prevailing in December 1972 cannot be characterized as a war crime; but he raised the question whether use of the B-52 was justified in view of the fact that "there were few military targets left." He saw the purpose of the bombing as, essentially, to "frighten the devil out of North Vietnam":

> This was primarily a psychological affair, to cause them such worry and anguish that they would hasten back to the negotiations. And that, of course, raises the question whether the purpose of the bombing is relevant when we talk about limitations.

Taylor cited other jurists who take the view that "you can only bomb for the purpose of hitting military objectives and you should not be allowed to bomb for political purposes." In reply, he said:

> It is a view which I must confess I find difficulty in accepting. One can't hear that without thinking of Clausewitz and the general idea that war is an extension of diplomacy and politics. Most people don't go to war just for the fun of war, but to achieve aims, and those aims are generally political.

I should emphasize that for Taylor the matter does not end there. He went on to raise the question whether bombing for the purpose of "terrorizing the population" (as distinct, presumably, from "killing the population") should be permissible. Still, his point that bombing for "political purposes" is legitimate, since wars themselves are fought for political purposes, seems eminently sensible and right.

7. The effectiveness of the Christmas bombing lay not in the amount of physical destruction it caused but in the psychological and political pressure it placed on the enemy. The *military* effect alone could probably have been achieved with considerably less bombing; the targets on the list released by U.S. authorities on December 28 could very likely have been put out of commission with less tonnage. It does indeed appear, as Taylor said, that the bombing was pursued largely for *psychological* purposes. And it achieved these purposes. The North Vietnamese were not so much hurt as impressed. The bombing was a message, and they got the message.

Whether President Nixon fully understood the effectiveness of the bombing in these terms is uncertain. In his memoirs he reports that on December 14 he called Admiral Thomas Moorer, chairman of the Joint Chiefs of Staff, and told him: "I don't want any more of this crap about the fact that we couldn't hit this target or that one. *This is your chance to use military power effectively to win this war,* and if you don't, I'll consider you responsible" (*RN,* p. 734; italics added). But the bombing of Hanoi and Haiphong was not a good example of what strategic bombing can accomplish. It did not inflict unacceptable military damage, and it certainly did not "win [the] war." By December 29 not only had the North Vietnamese run out of surface-to-air missiles, but U.S. forces had run out of plausible targets. One more day of bombing would have made the symbolic nature of the entire operation even more glaringly apparent.

As an invitation to resume serious negotiations, the bombing was not a subtle move; it was not a militarily effective move; it was certainly not a popular move; but it appears to have been a diplomatically effective one. Regrettably, this reality has never been acknowledged by the prestige press, which did so much to obscure the issues at the time. Acknowledgment of error does not come easily to human beings. It may come especially hard to leaders of the media, who sometimes operate as though they should be free from the criticism to which they subject the government and all other institutions in society.

# Kissinger's Statement On the Paris Talks
## December 16, 1972

*The following statement and excerpts from the question-and-answer period are from National Security Adviser Henry Kissinger's press conference in Washington as reported in the "New York Times" December 17, 1972 (subheads added).*

LADIES AND GENTLEMEN: As YOU KNOW, I have been reporting to the President and meeting with the Secretary of State, the Vice President, Secretary of Defense, Chairman of the Joint Chiefs, and other senior officials, and I'm meeting with you today because we wanted to give you an account of the negotiations as they stand today.

I'm sure you will appreciate that I cannot go into details of particular issues, but I will give you as fair and honest a description of the general trend of the negotiations as I can.

First let me do this in three parts: What led us to believe at the end of October that peace was imminent? Second, what has happened since? Third, where do we go from here?

At the end of October we had just concluded three weeks of negotiations with the North Vietnamese. As you all know, on October 8 the North Vietnamese presented to us a proposal which as it later became elaborated appeared to us to reflect the main principles that the President has always enunciated as being part of the American position.

These principles were that there had to be an unconditional release of American prisoners throughout Indochina.

Secondly, that there should be a cease-fire in Indochina, brought into being by various means suitable to the conditions of the countries concerned.

Third, that we were prepared to withdraw our forces under these conditions in a time period to be mutually agreed upon.

Fourth, that we would not prejudge the political outcome of the future of South Vietnam. We would not impose a particular solution. We would not insist on our particular solution.

The agreement as it was developed during October seemed to us to reflect these principles precisely.

Then towards the end of October we encountered a number of difficulties. Now at the time, because we wanted to maintain the atmosphere leading to a rapid settlement, we mentioned them at our briefings but we did not elaborate on them. But let me sum up what the problems were at the end of October.

It became apparent that there was in preparation a massive Communist effort to launch an attack throughout South Vietnam to begin several days before the cease-fire would have been declared and to continue for some weeks after the cease-fire came into being.

Second, there was an interview by the North Vietnamese prime minister which implied that the political solution that we had always insisted was part of our principles, namely, that we would not impose a coalition government, was not as clear-cut as our record of the negotiations indicated.

And thirdly, as no one could miss, we encountered some specific objections from Saigon.

### 'ONE MORE ROUND'

In these conditions we proposed to Hanoi that there should be one other round of negotiations to clear up these difficulties. We were convinced that with good will on both sides these difficulties could be relatively easily surmounted, and that if we conducted ourselves, on both sides, in the spirit of the October negotiations, a settlement would be very rapid. It was our conviction that if we were going to bring to an end ten years of warfare, we should not do so with an armistice, but with a peace that had a chance of lasting.

And therefore we proposed three categories of clarifications in the agreement:

First, we wanted the so-called linguistic difficulties cleared up so that they would not provide the seed for unending disputes and another eruption of the war. I will speak about those in a minute.

Secondly, the agreement always had provided that international machinery be put in place immediately after the cease-fire was declared. We wanted to spell out the operational meaning of the word "immediately" by developing the protocols that were required to bring the international machinery into being simultaneously with the cease-fire agreement. This, to us, seemed a largely technical matter.

And, thirdly, we wanted some reference in the agreement—however vague, however elusive, however indirect—which did not, which would make clear that the two parts of Vietnam would live in peace with each other and that neither side would impose its solution on the other by force.

These seemed to us modest requirements, relatively easily achievable.

Let me now tell you the sequence of events since that time.

We all know of the disagreements that have existed between Saigon and Washington. These disagreements are to some extent understandable. It is inevitable that a people on whose territory the war has been fought and that for twenty-five years has been exposed to devastation and suffering and assassination would look at the prospects of a settlement in a more, in a more detailed way and in a more anguished way than we who are 10,000 miles away.

Many of the provisions of the agreement, inevitably, were seen in a different context in Vietnam than in Washington. And I think it is safe to say that we faced, with respect to both Vietnamese parties, this problem. The people of Vietnam, North and South, have fought for so long that the risks and perils of war, however difficult, seem sometimes more bearable to them than the uncertainties and the risks and perils of peace.

Now it is no secret either that the United States has not agreed with all the objections that were raised by Saigon. In particular, the United States position with respect to the cease-fire had been made clear in October, 1970. It had been reiterated in the President's proposals of January 25, 1972. It was repeated again in the President's proposal of May 8, 1972. None of these proposals had asked for a withdrawal of North Vietnamese forces.

And therefore we could not agree with our allies in South Vietnam when they added conditions to the established position after an agreement had been reached that reflected these established positions.

And as was made clear in the press conference here on October 26, as the President has reiterated in his speeches, the United States will not continue the war one day longer than it believes is necessary to reach an agreement we consider just and fair. So, we want to leave no doubt about the fact that if an agreement is reached that meets the stated conditions of the President—if an agreement is reached that we consider just—that no other party will have a veto over our action.

But I am also—today this question is moot because we have not yet reached an agreement that the President considers just and fair. And therefore I want to explain to you the process of the negotiations since they resumed on November 20 and where we are. The three objectives that we were seeking in these negotiations were stated in the press conference of October 26, in many speeches by the President afterwards, and in every communication to Hanoi since. They could not have been a surprise.

## THE 'LINGUISTIC DIFFICULTIES'

Now let me say a word first about what were called linguistic difficulties, which were called these in order not to inflame the situation. How did they arise?

They arose because the North Vietnamese presented us a document in English which we then discussed with them, and in many places throughout this document the original wording was changed as the negotiations proceeded and the phrases were frequently weakened compared to the original formulation.

It was not until we received the Vietnamese text after those negotiations were concluded that we found that while the English terms had been changed the Vietnamese terms had been left unchanged, and so we suddenly found ourselves engaged in two negotiations, one about the English text, the other about the Vietnamese text.

Having conducted many negotiations, I must say this was a novel procedure, and it led to the view that perhaps these were not simply linguistic difficulties but substantive difficulties. Now I must say that all of these except one have now been eliminated.

## THE PROBLEM OF PROTOCOLS

The second category of problems concerned bringing into being the international machinery so that it could operate simultaneously with the cease-fire and so as to avoid a situation where the cease-fire rather than bring peace would unleash another frenzy of warfare. To that end we submitted on November 20, the first day that the negotiations resumed, a list of what are called protocols—technical instruments to bring this machinery into being.

These protocols—I will not go into the details of these protocols and they're normally technical documents—and ours were certainly intended to conform to normal practice despite the fact that this occurred four weeks after we had made clear that this was our intention and three weeks after Hanoi had pressed us to sign a cease-fire agreement. The North Vietnamese refused to discuss our protocols and refused to give us their protocols, so that the question of bringing the international machinery into being could not be addressed.

The first time we saw the North Vietnamese protocols was on the evening of December 12, the night before I was supposed to leave Paris, six weeks after we had stated what our end was, five weeks after the cease-fire was supposed to be signed—a cease-fire which called for this machinery to be set up immediately.

These protocols reopened—they're not technical instruments—but reopened a whole list of issues that had been settled—or we thought had been settled—in the agreement. They contained provisions that were not in the original agreement and they excluded provisions that were in the original agreement. They are now in the process of being discussed by the technical experts in Paris, but some effort will be needed to remove the political provisions from them, and to return them to a technical status.

Secondly, I think it is safe to say that the North Vietnamese perception of international machinery and our perception of international machinery is at drastic variance. And that, ladies and gentlemen, is an understatement.

We had thought that an effective machinery required, in effect, some freedom of movement. And our estimate was that several thousand people were needed to monitor the many provisions of the agreement.

The North Vietnamese perception is that the total force should be no more than 250, of which nearly half should be located at headquarters, that it would be dependent for its communication, logistics, and even physical necessities entirely on the party in whose area it was located. So it would have no jeeps, no telephones, no radios of its own; that it could not move without being accompanied by liaison officers of the party that was to be investigated—if that party decided to give it the jeeps to get to where the violation was taking place, and if that party would then let it communicate what it found.

It is our impression that the members of this commission will not exert themselves in frenzies of activity if this procedure were adopted.

Now, thirdly, the substance of the agreement. The negotiations since November 20 really have taken place in two phases: the first phase, which lasted for three days, continued the spirit and the attitude of the meetings in October. We presented our proposals—some were accepted, others were rejected. But by the end of the third day we had made very substantial progress. And we thought—all of us thought—that we were within a day or two of completing the arrangements.

## WITHIN REACH, BEYOND REACH

We do not know what decisions were made in Hanoi at that point, but from that point on the negotiations have had the character where a settlement was always just within our reach, and was always pulled just beyond our reach when we attempted to grasp it. I do not think it is proper for me to go into the details of the specific issues, but I think I should give you a general atmosphere and a general sense of the procedures that were followed.

When we returned on December 4, we were—we of the American team—thought that the meetings could not last more than two or three days because there were only two or three issues left to be resolved.

You all know that the meetings lasted nine days. They began with Hanoi withdrawing every change that had been agreed to two weeks previously. We then spent the rest of the week getting back to where we had already been two weeks before, and by Saturday we thought we had narrowed the issues sufficiently where, if the other side had accepted again one section that they had already agreed to two weeks previously, the agreement could have been completed.

At that point the President ordered General Haig to return to Washington so that he would be available for the mission that would then follow of presenting the agreement to our ally. At that point we thought we were sufficiently close so that experts could meet to conform the texts so that we would not again encounter the linguistic difficulties which we had experienced previously and so that we could make sure that the changes that had been negotiated in English would also be reflected in Vietnamese.

When the experts met they were presented with seventeen new changes in the guise of linguistic changes. When I met again with the special adviser, the one problem which we thought remained on Saturday had grown to two and a new demand was presented. When we accepted that it was withdrawn the next day and sharpened up. So we spent our time going through the seventeen linguistic changes and reduced them again to two.

Then on the last day of the meeting we asked our experts to meet to compare whether the fifteen changes that had been settled of the seventeen that had been proposed, whether those now conformed in the two texts. At that point we were presented with sixteen new changes, including four substantive ones, some of which now still remain unsettled.

Now I will not go into the details or into the merits of these changes. The major difficulty that we now face is that provisions that were settled in the agreement appear again in a different form in the protocols, that matters of technical implementation which were implicit in the agreement from the beginning have not been addressed and were not presented to us until the very last day of a series of sessions that had been specifically designed to discuss them, and that as soon as one issue was settled a new issue was raised.

It was very tempting for us to continue the process which is so close to everybody's heart implicit in the many meetings of indicating great progress. But the President decided that we could not engage in a charade with the American people.

And we are now in this curious position. Great progress has been made in the talks. The only thing that is lacking is one decision in Hanoi to settle the remaining issues in terms that two weeks previously they had already agreed to—so we are not talking of an issue of principle that is totally unacceptable—and secondly to complete the work that is required to bring the international machinery into being in the spirit that both sides have an interest of not ending the war in such a way that it is just the beginning of another round of conflict.

So we are in a position where peace can be near but peace requires a decision. And this is why we wanted to restate once more what our basic attitude is:

With respect to Saigon we have sympathy and compassion for the anguish of their people and for the concerns of their government. But if we can get an agreement that the President considers just we will proceed with it.

With respect to Hanoi our basic objective was stated in the press conference of October 26. We want an end of the war that is something more than an armistice. We want to move from hostilities to normalization and from normalization to cooperation. But we will not make a settlement which is a disguised form of continued warfare and which brings about by indirection what we have always said we would not tolerate.

We have always stated that a fair solution cannot possibly give either side everything that it wants. We have—we are not continuing a war in order to give total victory to our allies. We want to give them a reasonable opportunity to participate in a political settlement. But we also will not make a settlement which is a disguised form of victory for the other side.

Therefore we are at a point where we are again—perhaps we are closer to an agreement than we were at the end of October if the other side is willing to deal with us in good faith and with good will.

But it cannot do that every day an issue is settled a new one is raised, that when an issue is settled in an agreement it is raised again as an understanding and if it is settled in an understanding it is raised again as a protocol. We will not be blackmailed into an agreement. We will not be stampeded into an agreement. And, if I may say so, we will not be charmed into an agreement, until its conditions are right.

For the President, and for all of us who have been engaged in these negotiations, nothing that we have done has meant more than attempting to bring an end to the war in Vietnam. Nothing that I have done since I am in this position has made me feel more the trustee of so many hopes as the negotiations which I have—in which I have recently participated.

And it was painful at times to think of the hopes of millions—and indeed of the hopes of many of you ladies and gentlemen who were standing outside these various meeting places—expecting momentous events to be occurring, while inside one frivolous issue after another was surfaced in the last three days.

And so what we are saying to Hanoi is: We are prepared to continue in the spirit of the negotiations that were started in October. We are prepared to maintain an agreement that provides for the unconditional release of all American and allied prisoners, that imposes no political solution on either side, that brings about an internationally supervised cease-fire and the withdrawal of all American forces within sixty days.

It is a settlement that is just to both sides, and that requires only a decision to maintain provisions that had already been accepted, and an end to procedures that can only mock the hopes of humanity. And on that basis we can have a peace that justifies the hopes of mankind and the sense of justice of all participants.

## QUESTIONS AND ANSWERS

Now I'll be glad to answer some of your questions.

*Q. What do you think Hanoi's motive was in playing such a charade?*

A. I don't want to speculate on Hanoi's motives, and I have no doubt that before too long we will hear a version of events that does not exactly coincide with ours. I have attempted to give you as honest an account as I'm capable of. I believe—and this is pure speculation—that for a people that have fought for so long, it is paradoxically perhaps easier to face the risks of war than the uncertainties of peace. And it may be that they are waiting for a further accentuation of the divisions between us and Saigon, for more public pressures on us, or perhaps they simply cannot make up their minds.

*Q. Dr. Kissinger, from your account, one could conclude that the talks are now ended in terms of the series you have completed. Is that true? And, secondly, if it is not true, on what basis will they be resumed?*

A. We do not consider the talks completed. We believe that it would be a relatively simple matter to conclude the agreement because many of the issues that I mentioned in the press conference on October 26 have either been settled or substantial progress toward settling them has been made.

Therefore, if there were a determination to reach an agreement, it could be reached relatively quickly. On the other hand, the possibility of raising technical objections is endless. So if we have—as Le Duc Tho said yesterday—we would remain in contact through messages. We can then decide whether, or when, to meet again.

*Q. You have not discussed at all the proposals that the United States made on behalf of Saigon, which required changes in the existing agreement that had been negotiated. Can you discuss what they were and what effect they had on stimulating Hanoi—if they did—to making further proposals.*

A. As I pointed out, there were two categories of objections on the part of Saigon: objections which we agreed with, and objections which we didn't agree with.

The objections that we agreed with are essentially contained in the list that I presented at the beginning, and those were the ones we maintained. All of those, I believe, did not represent changes in the agreement but either clarifications, removal of ambiguities, or spelling out the implementation of agreed positions.

In the first sequence of meetings, between November 20 and November 26, most of those were—or many of those—were taken care of. So that we have literally—as I have pointed out before—been in the position where every day we thought it could and indeed almost had to be the last day.

The counterproposals that Hanoi had made were, again, in two categories. One set of changes that would have totally destroyed the balance of the agreement and which, in effect, withdrew the most significant concessions they had made. I did not mention those in my statement because in the process of negotiations they tended to disappear. They tended to disappear from the agreement, to reappear in understandings, and then to disappear from understandings to reappear in protocols. But I suspect that they will, in time, after the nervous exhaustion of our technical experts, disappear from the protocols as well.

But then there were a whole series of technical counterproposals which were absolutely unending and which hinged on such profound questions whether if you state an obligation in the future tense you were therefore leaving open the question when it would come into operation and whether you—a matter that reached the metaphysical at moments and which as soon as one of them was settled another one appeared and which made one believe that one was not engaged in an effort to settle fundamental issues but in a delaying action for whatever reason.

Now it is clear that the interplay between Saigon and Hanoi is one of the complicating features of this negotiation. But the basic point that we want to make clear is this: We have had our difficulties in Saigon. But the obstacle to an agreement at this moment is not Saigon because we do not as yet have an agreement that we can present to them.

*Q. Can an agreement be made operative without Saigon's signature?*

A. Well, this is a question that has not yet had to be faced but—and which we hope will not have to be faced.

*Q. Must there be, according to the President's terms, a substantial withdrawal of North Vietnamese troops from the South?*

A. The question of North Vietnamese forces in the South has two elements: the presence of the forces now there—it has three elements—the presence of the forces now there, their future, and the general claim that North Vietnam may make with respect to its right to intervene constantly in the South.

With respect to the last question, we cannot accept the proposition that North Vietnam has a right of constant intervention in the South. With respect to the first question of the forces now in the South, the United States has made three cease-fire proposals since October 1970, all of them based on the de facto situation as it existed at the time of the cease-fire, all of them approved by the government of South Vietnam, and therefore we did not add that condition of withdrawal to our present proposal, which reflected exactly the positions we had taken on January 25 and on May 9 of this year, both of which had been agreed to by the Government of the Republic of Vietnam.

*Q. Are we back to the beginning now in negotiations?*

A. No, we have an agreement that is 99 per cent completed as far as the text of the agreement is concerned. We also have an agreement whose associated implementations are very simple to conclude if one takes the basic provisions of international supervision that are in the text of the agreement, provisions that happen to be spelled out in greater detail in the agreement than almost any other aspect, and therefore we are one decision away from a settlement, and Hanoi can settle this any day by an exchange of messages after which there would be required a certain amount of work on the agreement which is not very much and some work in bringing the implementing instruments into being.

*Q. Could you tell us what that 1 per cent is?*

A. You know, I have found that I get into trouble when I give figures. Let me not insist on 1 per cent. It is an agreement that is substantially completed, but I cannot go into that. But that in any event is not the—that alone is not the problem.

*Q. Of what remains, would you describe it as fundamental or one of these technical problems? Because you've ranged between the two, I'm a little lost as to what is left.*

A. The technical implementing instruments that they have presented are totally unacceptable for the reasons which I gave. On the other hand, I cannot really believe that they are serious. What remains on the agreement itself is a fundamental point. It is, however, a point that has been accepted already two weeks previously and later withdrawn, so we are not raising a new fundamental point. We are raising the acceptance of something that had already once been accepted.

*Q. Is it political?*

A. I really don't want to go into the future of the Paris peace talks. I think that the sort of discussions that have been going on in the Paris peace talks are not affected by such temporary ups and downs as the private peace talks, so I'm sure that Minister Xuan Thuy and Ambassador Porter will find many subjects for mutual recrimination.

*Q. Isn't the fundamental point the one you raised about the right of North Vietnamese troops to intervene in the future of South Vietnam?*

A. I will not go into the substance of the negotiations.

*Q. It is the U.S. insistence that the two parts of Vietnam should live in peace with each other. Is that not the fundamental disagreement here?*

A. I can't consider it an extremely onerous demand to say that the parties of a peace settlement should live in peace with one another, and we cannot make a settlement which brings peace to North Vietnam and maintains the war in South Vietnam.

Q. *Isn't it that Vietnam is one country and this peace agreement is supposed to ratify that point?*

A. The question is whether their position isn't that Vietnam is one country and this agreement is supposed to ratify that point.

[*Another voice*] *This will be the final question as Henry has to leave now.*

A. I was wondering how he would conclude this thing.

Q. *Did you tell Hanoi ahead of time that you would talk to us?*

A. The answer to that is no, but I suspect you will get that message from them very quickly.

Q. *Was there any understanding in Paris before you left that each side would be free to express itself without damaging the possibility of future talks?*

A. Le Duc Tho correctly stated our agreement at the airport—that we would not go into the substance of the talks. Now I recognize that what I'm doing here goes to the edge of that understanding. But the President felt that we could not permit a situation to continue in which there was daily speculation as to something that was already accomplished while the record was so clearly contrary, and therefore we owed you an explanation not of the particular issues but of the progress of negotiations and exactly where they stood.

# North Vietnam's Statements
# On the Paris Talks
## December 17 and 21, 1972

*These three comments on the Kissinger press conference (see Appendix A) and the breakdown of negotiations were broadcast by the (North) Vietnam News Agency and recorded by the Foreign Broadcast Information Service.*

### 1   Broadcast in English, December 17; dateline Paris, December 16:

*Comments of Mr. Nguyen Thanh Le, spokesman for the Delegation of the Democratic Republic of Vietnam Government to the Paris Conference on Vietnam, on the statements made by Dr. Kissinger at his press conference on December 16, 1972.*

We would like to make the following preliminary remarks on the statements made by Dr. Kissinger at his press conference on December 16, 1972.

We have not yet the official full text of Dr. Kissinger's statements to the press. If the reports of the news agencies are correct, we feel it regrettable that the U.S. side has acted once again at variance with the agreement that both parties shall not publicly comment on the substance of the private talks between the Democratic Republic of Vietnam [DRV] and the United States.

Moreover, the U.S. side has deliberately distorted the fact, claiming that the DRV side had demanded changes to many questions and that it had thus created obstacles to the conclusion of the agreement. That is completely untrue.

It is known to everyone that in the October 20, 1972, message addressed on behalf of President Nixon to the Prime Minister of the DRV, the U.S. side acknowledged that the text of the agreement might be considered completed, and it proposed October 31, 1972, as the date for the signing of the agreement. Afterwards, the United States has insisted on changing many substantive questions, including many questions of principle.

The position of the DRV side is that the text of the agreement agreed upon on October 20, 1972, should be maintained. But if the U.S. side insists on changing it, our side will have also to propose necessary changes. The negotiations are

81

prolonged, the war increases its violence, [and] the responsibility for such a situation befalls on the U.S. side.

The Government of the DRV and the Vietnamese entire people have always desired a peaceful settlement of the Vietnam problem on the basis of respect for the fundamental national rights of the Vietnamese people and the right to self-determination of the South Vietnam population. The Vietnamese people will resolutely maintain their correct position and, at the same time, show their constant good will.

If the U.S. Government really desires to peacefully settle the Vietnam problem, respond to the aspirations of the American people and the world people, to ensure the American captured servicemen's early return to their families, and to repatriate all American soldiers participating in the war, it should sign the agreement agreed upon, without delay and without any change.

For its part, the DRV side will strictly respect the entire text of the agreement and is prepared to sign it with the U.S. side, the sooner the better.

## 2   Broadcast in Vietnamese, December 17 (translation):

Commenting on Kissinger's 16 December press conference, VNA [Vietnam News Agency] pointed out clearly that all attempts by the U.S. side to deceive public opinion and shrug off its responsibility will certainly be doomed.

On 16 December Kissinger, assistant to U.S. President Nixon for national security affairs, suddenly held a press conference to try to explain the reason why the United States had delayed signing the agreement on ending the war and restoring peace in Vietnam which it has reached with the DRV on 20 October.

In his speech as well as in his answers to newsmen, Kissinger held the DRV completely responsible for the negative results of the latest meetings in Paris and for the agreements not yet signed. While waiting to study the whole text of this press conference so we may have a more complete analysis, it is now necessary to stress again the basic truth of this matter. We can assert that Kissinger's justifications and denials at this press conference were completely untrue. No one can believe his effort to cast responsibility for the delay in the signing of the agreement on the DRV side.

Since 26 October everyone in the world has clearly seen that thanks to the good will and seriousness of the Vietnamese side, [the DRV Government,] with the concurrence of the PRGRSV [Provisional Revolutionary Government of the Republic of South Vietnam], initiated an important step by putting forth the draft of an agreement on ending the war and restoring peace to Vietnam. Everyone knows that this initiative was discussed in great detail, and later the delegates of the DRV Government and the U.S. Government approved the draft agreement on ending the war and restoring peace to Vietnam. U.S. President Nixon himself confirmed, in his message to the DRV premier late in October, that the text of the agreement might be considered complete, and proposed 31 October 1972 as the date for signing the agreement.

The DRV Government, in its 26 October statement, pointed out clearly how the Nixon administration had unilaterally delayed signing of the agreement and at the same time tried to soothe and deceive public opinion, saying that the remaining questions were only questions of technical details which could be solved in a new meeting of a few days.

Later the U.S. side proposed that the two sides meet again for further discussion, and twice the DRV side met the assistant to the U.S. President for national security affairs, on 20 November and on 4 December. This again showed maximum good will and the very serious attitude of our delegation. At a time when the U.S. side adopted an about-face attitude in delaying the signing of the agreement and demanding reexamination of many basic points of the agreement, Kissinger held a press conference in the United States which gave to the press a false interpretation of the facts and at the same time laid the blame at the door of the Vietnamese side. Nevertheless, all these attempts by the U.S. side can fool no one and can never succeed.

Everyone realizes that the DRV has always asserted its readiness to sign immediately the agreement agreed in the month of October 1972. Everyone also realizes that the U.S. Government has adopted a double-cross attitude toward the agreement, denied the U.S. President's confirmation that the text of the agreement was considered completed, and ignored the day for signing the agreement set forth by the U.S. President. Although Mr. Kissinger has repeatedly cast the blame on the DRV side, everyone knows that since the meeting of 20 November the U.S. side has insisted on changing a whole set of point, points which are basic and essential and have the force of principles and not linguistic, technical details and so forth.

Moreover, along with its negative attitude at the conference table, the U.S. administration has given puppet Nguyen Van Thieu free rein to oppose the agreement, in words and deeds, and has supplied the Saigon puppet administration with more weapons to step up the war and crack down more violently on the people under its control. More seriously, the U.S. side has also sought to strengthen the military apparatus in South Vietnam by sending tens of thousands of disguised military advisers to provide command for the Saigon army. In addition, it is using B-52 strategic bombers to lay waste to many populous areas in South Vietnam, including the areas surrounding Saigon. At the same time it is using U.S. air and naval forces to attack the DRV and B-52s to carpet-bomb many areas from Thanh Hoa to Vinh Linh zone.

It is thus clear that the United States has not given up its design to perpetuate its neocolonialist rule of South Vietnam, that it is striving to carry out its plan to Vietnamize the war there while prompting Nguyen Van Thieu to resist signing the peace agreement and even to reject the essentials of this agreement.

Whatever sophistry the United States may indulge in, it cannot avoid its responsibility for the present situation in the Vietnam peace talks. Its about-face attitude in demanding reexamination of the basic points of the agreement is the only obstacle to the agreement on ending the war and restoring peace in Vietnam, which thus far has not been signed.

Once again the DRV side seriously demands that the U.S. side adhere to the context of the agreement mutually agreed to on 20 October and sign that agreement without further delay. More than that, the U.S. side must see to it that the agreement, once signed, is implemented scrupulously so that there will be a lasting peace in Vietnam and the rest of Indochina.

### 3   Broadcast in English, December 21:

*At the 171st plenary session of the Paris conference on Vietnam this morning, Dinh Ba Thi, who deputized for the head delegation of the PRGRSV [Provisional Revolutionary Government of the Republic of South Vietnam] delegation, strongly denounced the Nixon administration for the extremely serious steps of war escalation it has made in the past few days against the whole territory of the DRV, and demanded the U.S. to put an immediate end to these criminal acts.*

*Refuting the U.S. distortions of the present state of negotiations, he pointed out:*
It is the U.S. side that has obstructed the talks. Washington has prompted Nguyen Van Thieu to make extremely absurd claims, which, in essence, is a revision of all the points agreed. The purpose is to blur the line between the United States—the aggressor—and the Vietnamese people, who resist it, and to deny the holy resistance of the South Vietnamese people and the PRGRSV, while making the U.S.-rigged administration "the only legitimate, constitutional" one. These claims are also meant to turn the temporary military demarcation line at the seventeenth parallel into a territorial boundary to perpetuate the partition of Vietnam, and South Vietnam into a separate state under the neocolonialist rule of the United States.

*After condemning the Nixon administration for pumping tens of thousands of tons of weapons and war means into South Vietnam, maintaining disguised military advisers and introducing new ones to continue providing command to the Saigon army, and making the Nguyen Van Thieu clique conduct one terror campaign after another against patriots and advocates of peace and national concord, Dinh Ba Thi pointed out:*
It is clear that the United States does not want peace. It is stepping up the "Vietnamization" policy and prolonging and expanding its involvement in Vietnam. An irrefutable proof of this is the hectic, reckless war escalation it is undertaking now.

*Dinh Ba Thi said in conclusion:*
The adventurous acts and war escalation of the United States will provoke due riposts and punishment from the entire Vietnamese people from the south to the north. The Vietnamese people want peace and independence and freedom. The more the United States prolongs and intensifies the war, the more resolutely the Vietnamese people, united millions as one man and closely siding with the brother peoples of Cambodia and Laos, will step up their war of resistance for national salvation, till complete victory.

*Nguyen Minh Vy, on behalf of the DRV delegation, said:*
It is public knowledge that although the United States has not kept its word by

not signing the agreement reached on October 20 at the date fixed for October 31 proposed by the United States itself, the DRV Government, as well-meaning as ever, continued to take part in the private meetings on the request of the United States. Yet, while the talks were going on, the U.S. side, on December 16, played a different tune, making groundless charges against the DRV side in an attempt to lay at the latter's door the blame for the obstruction of the talks. Immediately after that, the United States escalated the war against North Vietnam in an extremely serious manner, on an unprecedented scale, and with rare violence.

*Refuting the allegations made by the Nixon administration to justify the resumption of the bombing of North Vietnam, he pointed out:*

The intensification of the U.S. war is the logical sequel of what the United States has done in the past month—the delaying of the signing of the mutually reached agreement, the prolonging of the talks, the demand for a revision of the essential points of the agreement, the intensification of military operations against the liberation forces, the launching of many terror campaigns against the people, and the preparations for the sabotage of the agreement.

*Nguyen Minh Vy stressed:*

The DRV Government and the RSV Provisional Revolutionary Government have shown the maximum good will. If the United States opts for the path of peace, it must negotiate seriously, and promptly sign the agreement reached on October 20. Should the United States stubbornly continue the "Vietnamization" policy in South Vietnam and the bombing, mining, and blockading of North Vietnam, it would have to bear all the serious consequences of these criminal acts.

*After reading the text of his speech and proposing December 28 as the date for the next session, Nguyen Minh Vy declared:*

As a protest to the war escalation and the about-face of the United States in negotiations, the DRV Government delegation with the concurrence of the PRG Government declares the 171st session closed now.

*And the delegation of the DRV and that of the PRG walked out of the conference hall at 11:30 A.M. Paris time.*

# North Vietnam's Statement On the Bombing
## December 27, 1972

*This statement by the Foreign Ministry of the Democratic Republic of Vietnam was broadcast in English by the (North) Vietnam News Agency and recorded by the Foreign Broadcast Information Service.*

THE DRV FOREIGN MINISTRY TODAY ISSUED *the following statement regarding the extermination B-52 bombings conducted on the night of December 26 by the U.S. imperialists against many densely populated areas in the capital city of Hanoi, the port city of Haiphong and other places in North Vietnam:*
Continuing the frenzied war escalation against the DRV the U.S. imperialist aggressors on the night of December 26, 1972, again sent many flights of B-52 strategic bombers and dozens of other planes for extermination bombings against many areas inside and around Hanoi, in Haiphong city, Thai Nguyen city, and many other places. These are brutal acts aimed at massacring civilians, a crime that far exceeds in barbarity the ones perpetrated in the past by the Hitlerite fascists.

By conducting B-52 carpet-bombings and indiscriminate raids by other aircraft against the densely populated areas, the Nixon administration has inflicted thousands of casualties and destroyed thousands of houses and dozens of medical stations, including the Bach Mai hospital, one of the longest-standing centers for medical research in North Vietnam, many schools, including the Economic and Planning College and the Polytechnics in Hanoi, many cultural works, many public utility installations, etc. U.S. bombs and rockets have also caused damage to eight embassies in Hanoi and a number of foreign ships anchored at Haiphong harbor.

While frantically escalating the war, the Nixon administration is attempting to deceive public opinion with endless contentions about its "desire to negotiate seriously" and "to find out at an early date a solution to the war" while, in fact, resorting to acts of war escalation to block the road to a settlement. The Nixon administration pretends that it is concerned about the captured U.S. military men and doing everything to bring them home, while, by massive bombings, threatening the fact [*sic*] the lives and living conditions of hundreds of U.S. pilots being detained and further lengthening the list of captured U.S. military men.

The Nixon administration's international brigandage acts and policy to negotiate on a position of strength have aroused profound hatred among the Vietnamese people and high indignation among the world people. The whole progressive mankind is unanimously raising its voice to demand the Nixon administration to stop immediately the current frantic war escalation step against the DRV.

Let the U.S. imperialist aggressors harbor no illusion about subduing the heroic Vietnamese nation by the force of bombs and shells. The U.S. aggressors will certainly be duly punished for every step of their war escalation. On the night of December 26, 1972, the armed forces and people in Hanoi, Haiphong, and Thai Nguyen fought valiantly and staunchly, and shot down eight B-52s and wiped out or captured many American pilots. All in all, in more than a week, the armed forces and people of North Vietnam have shot down sixty-two U.S. aircraft including twenty-six B-52s and wiped out or captured many air pirates. This is an ignominious failure of the U.S. imperialist aggressors, and a big victory of our people.

So long as the Nixon administration pursues its brutal war policy, the Vietnamese people will resolutely carry out the testament of venerated President Ho Chi Minh, persist in and promote their fight against U.S. aggression, for national salvation in the military, political, and diplomatic fields till total victory so as to liberate the south, defend and build up the socialist north, and proceed toward a peaceful reunification of the country. The Vietnamese people are resolved to stand shoulder to shoulder with the brother peoples of Laos and Cambodia, further tighten their ranks, and promote the fight so as to drive the U.S. imperialists out of the Indochinese peninsula, and regain national independence and freedom for each country.

The Government of the Democratic Republic of Vietnam once again severely denounces to world public opinion the new, extremely serious step of war escalation taken by the U.S. imperialist aggressors against North Vietnam. It resolutely demands that the Nixon administration put an end to the bombardments, the blockade, and all other acts of encroachment upon the sovereignty and security of the DRV, stop its aggressive war in Vietnam, and give up its "Vietnamization of the war" policy.

The Government of the Democratic Republic of Vietnam and the Vietnamese people thank the governments and peoples of the other socialist countries, the governments and peoples of the peace- and justice-loving countries in the world, the various international organizations, and the American people for having timely and firmly condemned the Nixon administration's frenzied war acts. The DRV Government and the Vietnamese people earnestly call on their friends in all the five continents to continue to struggle in order to check the bloodstained hands of the U.S. imperialist aggressors, who are deliberately massacring civilians and exterminating towns and populous areas in the DRV, and to lend stronger support to the Vietnamese people's just cause till complete victory.

APPENDIX D

# *"Terror From the Skies"*
## A New York Times *Editorial*
## *December 22, 1972*

ASKED WHETHER CIVILIAN CENTERS would not inevitably be hit during the resumed massive air assault on North Vietnam, a Pentagon spokesman replied, "No, we do not strike civilian targets." He then amended his comment to say: "We do not target civilian targets."

The difference is crucial.

The big B-52 bombers that are being used for the first time over the heavily populated Hanoi-Haiphong area are not precision weapons. Normally they operate in flights of three that lay down a pattern of bombs—twenty tons to a plane—which scatter over an area more than half a mile wide and more than a mile and a half long.

Even if the "targets" were strictly military, a great deal more than military would inevitably be caught up in such sweeping devastation, especially in a blitz that in the first two days is estimated to have dropped 20,000 tons of explosives—the equivalent of the Hiroshima bomb. Imagine what would happen to New York or any other American city if a comparable enemy were unleashed to attack such targets on the Pentagon's authorized list as railyards, shipyards, command and control facilities, warehouse and transshipment areas, communications facilities, vehicle-repair facilities, power plants, railway bridges, railway rolling stock, truck parks, air bases, air-defense radars, and gun and missile sites.

It requires no horror stories from Hanoi radio to deduce that the destruction and human suffering must be very extensive indeed. And to what end?

Officials in Washington and Saigon have suggested that the raids are intended to disrupt a Communist offensive. But military men in Saigon say they have seen no indication that the North Vietnamese are preparing for such a strike.

Administration spokesmen have also reported that this brutal assault is intended to convey to North Vietnamese leaders President Nixon's displeasure over Hanoi's intransigence at the Paris peace talks. Only last week, however, a responsible American official in Paris indicated that the impasse centered on President Thieu's insistence, backed by President Nixon, that any agreement specifically recognize Saigon's authority over all of South Vietnam. This amounts to a demand that the Communists acknowledge a defeat they have not suffered on the battlefield.

No matter who is to blame for the breakdown in talks, the massive, indiscriminate use of the United States' overwhelming aerial might to try to impose an American solution to Vietnam's political problems is terrorism on an unprecedented scale, a retreat from diplomacy which this nation would be the first and loudest to condemn if it were practiced by any other major power. In the name of conscience and country, Americans must now speak out for sanity in Washington and peace in Indochina.

# "*Terror Bombing In the Name of Peace*"
## *A Washington Post Editorial December 28, 1972*

HOW DID WE GET IN A FEW short weeks from a prospect for peace that "you can bank on," in the President's words, to the most savage and senseless act of war ever visited, over a scant ten days, by one sovereign people upon another? And perhaps more to the point, what is the logic and where are the lessons of history that say we can run this reel backward after a time and proceed from terror bombing to "peace"—that there is, in other words, some rational cause and effect here, running either way?

The sad, hard answer is that while there are few conclusive lessons from history in this matter, the supposed "logic" of proceeding from bargaining to bombing and back to bargaining, in the name of peace, has been fundamental to this country's Vietnam strategy of "limited war" by "graduated response" over more than eight years and two administrations. In the beginning, it was accepted, with precious little protest, by Democrats and Republicans alike; and it was quietly acquiesced in by a good many of the people who now talk of "genocide" and "war crimes" and of the intolerable "immorality" of our current policy.

That we recite this background is in no way to suggest that we think Mr. Nixon is somehow mandated to continue to compound past follies. On the contrary, having promised us so many times to end this war within his first four years and having failed so dismally, for all that he might have learned from recent history, he is under greater obligation than any of his predecessors were to re-evaluate the mission, to reassess our capabilities, to recognize our limitations—and to change our strategy. But the change that is needed is not likely to be encouraged by denouncing the horror now unfolding in the skies over North Vietnam as something entirely new and different and essentially Nixonian. If this strategy is contrary to all we hold sacred, it would seem to follow that in some measure it always was. In short, we are not going to find it easy to work our way out of a ten-year-old war effort that has demonstrably failed of its early high hopes unless

---

we are prepared to begin by admitting that this is so; that we are all caught up, in one degree or another, with the responsibility for a war plan gone horribly wrong; that this country undertook an enterprise it could not handle, at least in any time frame and at any expenditure of lives and resources worthy of the objective; and that it would be the mark of a big power to cut our losses and settle for the only reasonable outcome that we now must know could ever have been realistically expected.

We should begin, in other words, not simply by shouting about the immorality of what we are now doing, but by first acknowledging the tragic impracticality of what we set out to do, and the enormity of the miscalculations and misjudgments that have been made, however honestly, from the very start. For only from this admission can we proceed rationally to deal with the monumental contradiction in the administration's current strategy. The contradiction begins with the administration's seeming insistence on a fully-enforceable, guaranteed settlement of the war on the old, familiar, original terms—"freedom" and "independence" and "enduring peace" for South Vietnam; anything seriously short of that, Mr. Nixon would have us believe, would be abject surrender, the abandonment of an ally, and a "stain upon the honor" of the United States.

Leaving aside the clichés which have come to be so inevitably a part of every serious presentation of our policy, there are two things tragically wrong about this statement of our aims, and the first is that such objectives are demonstrably unobtainable. The violent and embittered conflict that has engulfed Indochina for several decades is not going to be "settled" by any piece of paper that Dr. Henry Kissinger could conceivably persuade both North and South Vietnam to sign. That is the loud lesson of the collapse of the last peace plan; it asked too much of a situation which can only be resolved in ambiguity. Such is the conflict of purpose on both sides, in fact, that it can fairly be said that in negotiating a "settlement" we are in fact merely writing the rules of engagement for a continuing struggle for control of South Vietnam by other less openly military means.

So we are not talking about "peace," and still less about "abandoning an ally," for there can be no resolution of the fighting which will not present each side both with risks and with opportunities of losing—or winning—in large measure what each has been fighting for. To pretend that we are doing otherwise—that we are making "enduring peace" by carpet-bombing our way across downtown Hanoi with B-52s—is to practice yet one more cruel deception upon an American public already cruelly deceived. It is, in brief, to compound what is perhaps the real immorality of this administration's policy—the continuing readiness to dissemble; to talk of "military targets" when what we are hitting are residential centers and hospitals and commercial airports; to speak of our dedication to the return of our POWs and our missing in action even while we add more than seventy to their number in little more than a week.

We think the American people could face the truth of how little there is we can really count on accomplishing in Vietnam—if they were to hear it from the President. But we have not heard from the President—not since "peace was at hand." Instead, we have heard from surrogates and spokesmen and military headquarters, cryptically, about the loss of men and aircraft and the alleged military significance of the raids. It is from others, around the world, that we hear about the havoc our bombers are wreaking on innocent civilians with the heaviest aerial onslaught of this or any other war. All this we are presumably doing to redeem the "honor of America," and this is the second part of what's wrong—and contradictory—about the President's bombing policy. For it is hard to envisage any settlement that we could realistically hope to negotiate which could justify the effort now being expended to achieve it or wash away the stains on this country's honor of the past ten days.

# Commentary by Eric Sevareid
## CBS Evening News
## December 29, 1972

AN INNOVATION OF THIS administration has been the annual state-of-the-world message. Last winter this Nixon-Kissinger document said: "Vietnam no longer distracts our attention from the fundamental issues of global diplomacy or diverts our energies from priorities at home." That is the way it was beginning to look then. There were the giant steps taken toward China and Russia, and the relentless peace negotiations in Paris in an atmosphere of drama, then elation, then nothing.

The year ends in the starkest of contrasts with a graphic demonstration of the two deep-seated paradoxical streams in the American political temper which so puzzles the world—kindness and belligerence. The President has ordered an all-out effort to save the lives of the stricken people of Managua right after his order for an all-out bombing of Vietnam's industrial base, which has to mean the mass killing of civilians. How many we do not know, but a government study three years ago estimated that at the peak of our bombing of North Vietnam in previous years, about a thousand people were killed or injured each week. The most intensive bombing campaigns in that '65-'68 period did not match the intensity of the current campaign.

Congressmen are beginning to filter back to Washington, and their questions are now filling the news vacuum here. Is it possible to get what the President calls an honorable peace by dishonorable means? How is it possible to preserve American leadership and credibility in the world, which the President says is the important goal, when the moral base for that national posture is being hacked away? When Mr. Nixon speaks out, as he will have to do soon, we may all know more than we do about what went wrong and what options remain.

If productive negotiations are not resumed, three alternatives occur to observers here. One is more punishing of North Vietnam. The second is just to get out with no negotiated agreement at all, keeping air power in Thailand and offering economic help to Hanoi in a carrot-and-stick approach to get the prisoners home. And it may be significant that certain writers who have generally approved the administration line are now suggesting this, even though we've all been told for years that a negotiated political settlement was the only way. The third conceivable alternative is for the President to let the Congress take the ball and the problem away from him by voting to cut off the war funds.

There will be such a congressional effort in any case. Already some senators are resurrecting an old and basic point—arguing that the President has no legal authority for making war. The Tonkin Gulf resolution has been repealed. The authority the President has been going on is the inherent right of the Commander-in-Chief to protect American troops. Very few such troops remain in Vietnam, and the connection between their safety and the Hanoi bombing has not been established.

# "*About the Bombing*"
## A Wall Street Journal *Editorial*
## *December 27, 1972*

WE THINK THERE ARE CERTAIN pointed questions to be asked about the renewed bombing of North Vietnam, but it seems to us intelligent questioning ought to start by recognizing that Mr. Nixon was right about Cambodia and right about Haiphong.

The invasion of the Cambodian sanctuaries, so widely and wildly decried at the time, speeded the now nearly complete withdrawal of American ground troops. The mining of Haiphong and associated bombings in the North helped, when combined with the peaceful overtures to Peking and Moscow, to bring North Vietnam into the first truly serious negotiations of the war. In both cases the President's bold military gambles ultimately contributed not to expanding the war but to winding it down. Thus it seems to us foolish to dismiss entirely the possibility that he may be lucky a third time.

Many of the President's critics made up their minds in 1967 and have not been paying attention since. So their starting premise is not that the Haiphong mining and bombing worked, but that bombing is an utterly discredited and worthless instrument. Anyone starting with this premise proceeds naturally to "barbarism," "stone-age," "shame," and the other tiresome rhetoric we have heard this last week. Of course the bombing is immoral if the first given condition is that it has no hope of speeding the end of the war. But whether it will speed the end of the war is not a "given" but the issue itself.

After all that is said, of course, there remains plenty of room for questioning. One pertinent line of inquiry concerns the precise rationale for the bombing. The administration has been exceptionally silent on this issue, and the bombings came so suddenly even some of the usual supporters are wondering whether in fact there is a cogent rationale behind them, or whether they are chiefly an expression of frustration.

Especially so since, contrary to the style of Mr. Nixon's previous military moves, the presumed purpose of the raids cannot be accomplished unilaterally. The invasion of Cambodia neutralized the sanctuaries, the mining of Haiphong closed the port, regardless of the Communist reaction. Success in the new bombings depends on a reaction from Hanoi, namely the return to serious negotiation. What will Mr. Nixon do if this reaction is not forthcoming? Have the raids foreclosed more options than they have opened?

A second and even more important line of questioning concerns American purposes at this juncture. At his press conference just before the bombing was resumed, Henry Kissinger talked quite a bit about wanting a settlement that is "more than an armistice," and refusing one that is "a disguised form of continued warfare." We wonder whether this represents an escalation of American purposes in the concluding stages of the war.

Is the purpose actually to settle the war and bring peace to Indochina? Is that why the bombing is necessary? We have usually taken the objective of Mr. Nixon's Vietnamization policy to be securing an honorable American exit from the war, with the ultimate outcome to be determined by some kind of struggle between the Vietnamese parties. We have thought, and continue to think, that an objective of guaranteeing peace is an unrealistic one, given the history of the conflict, and by far an overly ambitious one, given the cost of the war to American society.

It's easy to put too fine a point on this difference, of course, since any negotiations that would allow an American exit would inevitably become involved with the ground rules for an ensuing struggle. And even Mr. Kissinger told us relatively little about the background of negotiation that provides the context for the renewed bombing. Lacking knowledge of the details of that background, we find ourselves not so much distraught as puzzled, not condemning but questioning.

The negotiations came so close to a settlement of the war these past few months it is almost unimaginable it will now slip away, or would be almost unimaginable were it not for the long history of tragedy in Vietnam. We can only hope that the latest bombing is not the opening of a new chapter in that tragedy but a step in the dénouement of the old one. Mr. Nixon's success with his first two gambles suggests that hope is not an impossible one, but we certainly pray that his luck does not turn sour the third time around.

APPENDIX H

# "The Peace That Wasn't"
**From The Economist (London)**
**December 23, 1972**

THERE IS NO REASON THAT A LIBERAL should accept why the two Viet-
nams ought to be reunited until it has been shown that a majority of the people in
both of them, or at least of those in the south, wish it to be so. Until that happens, a
liberal would add, South Vietnam should have a government of its own based on
some sort of reasonably accurate measurement of the preferences of the South
Vietnamese. Most people in the west would accept those principles; after all, it is
what they say about that other divided nation, Germany, and they would be
outraged if one half of Germany sent its army into the other half in order to insist
on putting its own preferred sort of government into power there. The difference
in Vietnam is the reluctance of so many people to apply these principles as the
necessary test of the terms on which the war is ended. It was imprecision in
applying this test that led Mr. Kissinger to say on October 26th that "peace is at
hand," when it turns out that it was not. The same imprecision is now making
many bone-weary people say that he could nevertheless embrace in December
the consequences of what he let his eye slide over too easily in October.

By sending his bombers back north of the twentieth parallel this week, and
losing quite a lot of them, President Nixon has reverted to the argument of force to
end the war. He is using the means at his disposal, as the North Vietnamese used
the means at their disposal when they sent their army over the seventeenth
parallel in the spring. They employed the firepower carried by their army; he is
using the firepower of his air force. The pictures from An Loc and Quang Tri show
that there is not much difference between them in what they do to the places
where the artillery shells or the bombs fall. But there is a fundamental difference,
and it should be recognized, between the purposes for which Mr. Nixon and the
North Vietnamese politburo are using the different sorts of power available to
them. Mr. Nixon is using the argument of force to try to get the North Vietnamese
to agree that the next government of South Vietnam should be chosen by a more
or less violence-free election. The North Vietnamese are using their sort of force
to try to insist that that government should itself be the product of the further
violence which they and their friends in the south would bring to bear after a

Reprinted by permission from *The Economist,* London, December 23, 1972.

97

nominal ceasefire. These are the two very different meanings that lay concealed beneath the skin of the agreement that seemed so close in October.

Mr. Kissinger, and those who hoped he was right, had their eyes fixed on the passage in clause 4 of the agreement which said that "the internal matters" of South Vietnam were to be settled between "the two South Vietnamese parties." By saying that, North Vietnam seemed to be renouncing its own claim to decide what should happen in the south; and if the North Vietnamese kept out of it all there was little doubt that the non-communists would win a large majority in the election President Thieu has long been offering to hold after the ceasefire. It is true, of course, that clause 1 of the agreement paid due respect to the unity of Vietnam. But it was hoped that that was the equivalent of the letter the west Germans have sent to the east Germans about German unity, a formal but at the moment non-operative reminder of their right to bring the subject up again later on. If North Vietnam carried out its promise (clause 7) to withdraw its troops from Laos and Cambodia, and if its men in South Vietnam had a real team of truce supervisors watching over them, it seemed that the North Vietnamese army could be more or less neutralised. And from 1965 onwards the removal of the North Vietnamese intervention has been the main argument used to justify the American intervention.

That was the pattern Henry Kissinger thought he saw in the agreement, but Le Duc Tho plainly saw a different one. It has been known for some time—from Cosvn-6, the document the communist headquarters issued in mid-September— that the Vietcong has been telling its men to organise undercover squads for a campaign of "tyrant elimination, abduction and assassination" after the ceasefire. Mr. Thieu's army and police force could probably cope with that if North Vietnam's fourteen regular divisions really did stay out of the war. But the sort of international inspection system the North Vietnamese turn out to have been calling for makes it highly unlikely that they ever intended to stay out of it. They apparently proposed a total of 250 men for the whole of Indochina, only half of whom would actually be allowed to travel around the countryside, and even those few would have had to rely for transport on the people they wanted to inspect.

## TWO STATES IN ONE NATION

It would be a bad joke, if the old control commission set up in 1954 had not stopped people laughing about supervisors who supervise nothing. Such a handful of inspectors could not possibly know what General Giap's men were doing in South Vietnam, let alone check that they had got out of Laos and Cambodia. This is not the proposal of men who, in the Guardian's bland phrase on Wednesday, "know that they . . . cannot win." It seems only too likely that North Vietnam's leaders wanted nobody watching their army while it pursued its own definition of victory in the south after the last American had left. The question of the supervisory force is not in itself the one last decision that Mr. Kissinger says the North Vietnamese still have to take. That decision is to leave the politics of the south to the southerners, within the procedures already agreed to in October; but the powers of the supervisors are a decisively important test of whether North Vietnam is really ready for that.

What Mr. Nixon is still trying to get is the Vietnamese version of what Herr Brandt has settled for in Germany—the acceptance by North Vietnam's leaders that there are "two states within one nation." The North Vietnamese went part of the way to accepting that in October, when they dropped the idea that the United States should remove Mr. Thieu from power, and put a coalition government in his place, before they would agree to a ceasefire. But they will still be evading the central issue so long as they refuse to accept any real limitations on what their army can do after a ceasefire. Perhaps they are trying to take advantage of the difficult moment Mr. Nixon has created for himself just before Christmas, by allowing the expectations of peace to outrun reality and the wives and mothers to think that the American prisoners were as good as home. Perhaps they believe that the new Senate, with two more Democrats in it, will cut off funds for the war. But they know that, if that does not happen, Mr. Nixon is pretty well free from political constraints at home until 1974 or 1975, when he will want to start making his preparations for America's bicentenary; and although he is not going to make it his policy to bomb them back into the stone age—that brutal phrase used years ago by one foolish American general, and so often put into other Americans' mouths since then—he can cause a great deal of damage to North Vietnam. They have their calculations to make.

## THE BREZHNEV CALCULATION

So do the Russians. What happens now will be a measure of whether there really is a new relationship between the Soviet Union and the United States. It is Russian-supplied missiles, and Russian training in using them, that shot down six B-52s by Thursday; since the B-52s seemed almost invulnerable until recently, it is even possible that the equipment which brought them down was sent into North Vietnam during the two-month halt of bombing north of the twentieth parallel. It is almost certainly Russian oil pumped in over the Chinese border that keeps North Vietnam's war machine in action.

There is assumed to be a tacit understanding between Mr. Nixon and Mr. Brezhnev. If the United States provides the help that Russia needs to overcome the inefficiency of its economy, and underwrites the political division of Europe, the assumption is that the Soviet Union will help, among other things, to end the Vietnam war in a way compatible with Mr. Nixon's definition of peace with honour. It is hard to imagine Mr. Nixon quietly proceeding with his part of that understanding if the Russians continue to help the North Vietnamese to make the other part impossible: if the centrepiece of Mr. Nixon's second term has to be a choice between continued war in Vietnam and the acceptance of defeat. That is not how Mr. Nixon wanted his next four years to be. The Vietnam war stretches out its consequences into many parts of the world. That is why it has been so long and terrible a war, and why it is so difficult to end; and why Mr. Brezhnev, on reflection, may not choose to use it as a rug to whip from under Mr. Nixon's feet.

# Index of Names

*Note:* This index was prepared by Richard E. Sincere.

# Ethics and Public Policy Reprints

**Reprints are $1 each. Postpaid if payment accompanies order.**
**Orders of $10 or more, 10 per cent discount.**